a short statement. It's got to be a book.

Job said, "What I feared has come upon me; and what I dreaded has happened to me." (Job 3:25)

For some time now I have been suspended in a cloud of uncertainty. In 2014, sitting in a consultation room at Norton Cancer Institute in Louisville, KY; the doctor, who just an hour before had taken a biopsy from a knot in the back of my right leg; walked into the room with his nurse practitioner and said to me, "You have cancer; and it is a some type of sarcoma." I had no idea what that would turn out to be. I do know that those words were harder to hear than I had ever imagined. I felt like bawling. I choked back the tears and tried to stifle my emotions that were about to rupture. I didn't want to lose it right there in front of the doctor; but also I wanted to be strong and not break down with my wife sitting next to me, who also was fighting hard against the urge to cry. That began a whole new journey for me, my wife and children, my mom and dad, brothers and sisters, and also an entire congregation of beloved brothers and sisters from the church where I pastor, and many others who know and love me who are part of my family in

Christ elsewhere.

After surgery in October, the primary tumor was successfully removed, and I was sent home to recover. Soon appointments were set up to do follow up screenings every three months. The first three month checkup was supposed to go off without a hitch. It didn't. The doctor reviewed my scans and said that I had three tiny nodules in my lungs. "Probably nothing. Shouldn't worry at this point. We will look at them again in three months." That began a cycle of scans, suspicious nodules and more questions. Unfortunately, my three nodules turned into six, and then ten.

As some of you know I have been going to CTCA (Cancer Treatment Centers of America) for my monitoring. My doctors at CTCA initially met with me and looked at my reports, did a few tests of their own and confirmed what my doctor in Louisville had said, The nodules are too small to biopsy or take out; so we'll just have to watch you. Then I began to have some back problems. I developed pains in my lower back. I mentioned this to my doctor at CTCA and she ordered an MRI. The results of that test revealed a bulging disc in my lower back; but much more concerning, there was a small lesion in my L2 vertebrae. The doctor said repeatedly over several months that it was nothing to worry about. So, I asked her if she could tell my why she wasn't worried, so I could "not worry" along with her. She said that there are about a hundred things that the lesion could be; "cancer being one of them." She was not suspicious of cancer at that point. To make a long story shorter, my primary care doctor at home was not satisfied with the approach my doctor at CTCA was taking. It was bothering me too that the CTCA oncologist was being dismissive of the lesion and not investigating it further, since I was a cancer patient with tiny nodules in my lungs. My primary care doctor set up an appointment for a second opinion. So recently I have gone to Vanderbilt where the doctor looked over all my reports, scans, and did some of her own. A biopsy was suggested to determine clinically what the spine lesion was, though she was 90% sure that the nodules in my lungs were Leiomyosarcoma. Before a biopsy, a PET scan was ordered to see if there might be anything else that appeared in other parts of my body. Since I had not heard from the doctor about the PET scan results, I went to have the biopsy done on my spine, thinking that everything else was clear. I was wrong. There was a tumor in my right pelvic area. Well to get to the point, they took a biopsy from the tumor in my hip. This past Tuesday I met with the oncologist at Vanderbilt who confirmed that I have metastatic Leiomyosarcoma in my lungs, spine and right pelvic area. She suggested that I start chemo right away; but she was aware that I was not wanting to do chemo. So, after I declined chemo, she said that I have some time to wait, and if I changed my mind, we could start it later, especially since I'm not manifesting any symptoms beyond some lower back pain. I did ask the question that everyone in that situation wants to know, the How long do I have question. Given my stage of cancer and its spread, she said that I could have one year; perhaps five, or even possibly ten. It all depends on how fast the cancer grows. With that, the plan is to go back in 4 months for scans to monitor the growth of the metastases. She said there was no need to subject me to lots of scans if I'm not doing chemo. She said that whatever my decision was that she would support me; and if I did not want chemo, she would help me with management. Essentially, this is terminal. Truth is, chemo can't save me. It might be true that the chemo could add some time to my life. However, I have witnessed so many people down through my ministry who've had cancer, chemo, and in the end, there was no great benefit, but in many cases, suffering was increased tremendously. If I don't have much time left, then I want to hold on to as much quality time as I can, as opposed to being sick a little longer. So, in a nut shell; I have terminal cancer in my lungs, spine and bones. However…

I'm not done yet!

The day before my doctor appointment I was talking with my dad. He said something to the effect that whatever the doctor says, it's not the last word. I replied to him, "Well, I'm not going down to Vanderbilt to talk to God. I'm going to talk to a doctor." I have witnessed the hand of God moving in impossible situations, and making things that could not happen, happen! This situation is no different.

When Moses and the children of Israel were cornered at the Red Sea, God did the impossible and parted the waters. When David went out onto the battlefield as a young boy to face down a giant, God did the impossible, and the boy became a giant killer. When three of the Hebrews were thrown into the fiery furnace for not bowing down and worshipping and image of gold, God did the impossible, and went into the fire with them. The didn't burn or even break out in a sweat! There was a fourth man walking in the fire with them. They came out without a sing or even the smell of smoke. I could go on for hours telling about the impossible things that God has done easily. I know that Leiomyosarcoma is formidable for me. But it doesn't stand a chance against God!

At this point, many people are praying. Many of you have been, and continue to pray. I am so grateful... I would ask for your continued prayers. Also, I am beginning a search for alternative options that might be available. To be honest with you; I have no idea whether they will work or not: but God does! I do know that He alone is the healer. So, this is my plan.

I am appealing my case before the Supreme Court of heaven. I understand that I am on the King's docket! He is hearing my case, and will soon make a final ruling! I have never known Him to make a wrong judgment, be unkind, mean, disinterested, or wanting upfront money.

The Judge is also speaking to the Great Physician about my condition! Jesus has and always will be my physician and Lord! He brought me into this world. He has watched over me all my life. He helped my family through the loss of my older brother Stephen when he was killed two weeks before his 14th birthday in May of 1978. That was a hard time. But Jesus was there with us. He's watched over me through all my illnesses, hardships, trials, sufferings, and I have never known Him to make a misdiagnosis, or write a wrong prescription, or take a vacation, or to be unavailable. I will admit, when I have gone to see Him in His office, I have had to wait; sometimes, a long time in the waiting room. But, that's alright. It's not just good for the doctor to have patients. It is good also for the patient to have patients. It's all part of the answer. You can be sure that when my name comes up and I'm called in to find out what the ruling is; it will be right, and good! I also have learned that a special investigator has been dispatched to look into my case. You're not going to believe it; He is my attorney, my advocate! He's also my best Friend: more than even my blood brothers; and believe me, we're tight. He has been hovering over me, and when I speak to Him about my case, His assurance is that I can't lose. "Listen," He tells me, "There is no way you can lose this case." How can I? I win either way!

The only adversary I have in this is the devil. Surely he must not know it, but the Judge is also my Father. Satan is so stupid. Not only is the Judge my Father, but Jesus, my Savior, Lord, and Friend is pleading my case at the Father's right hand. Satan might able to accuse, and so I say, "Let er' blow!" He's a windbag anyway. Always when he appears before the Judge, it is with lies and accusations and a scowl. I don't think He will be able to persuade the Judge (my Father God), my Physician (Jesus, Lord of all), and my Attorney and advocate (the Holy Spirit).

Oh, but there is one thing that will help in my case, and this is where you come in. It seems that witnesses to speak in my behalf will definitely help: and that's you. If you could; you don't have to take time off work to do it, or even get out of bed. You don't have to leave what you're doing to appear in court, just pray. Yep, that's it! Pray! Praying is accepted in heaven's court as evidence, when it is prayed in Jesus' name. So with that, I'm asking for your prayers as I take on the fight of my life, for my life. There are some things that I would like for you to pray for specifically.

To live (only if it is the Lord's will)

My wife and children, family and my church (This is so very hard for all of us)

Wisdom (to make wise and good choices that might assist me and my family in this battle.

One final note and I'll let you go to bed. If you're not

tired, I am. I'm also looking into clinics outside of the US that have various therapies that are not available here. I'm looking into supplements that individually might not be that expensive, but together and over time would be burdensome. I am also looking into setting up a fundraising effort to help and be able to afford these or other options.

God tells us in His word that He will feed us, if we seek first the kingdom of God and His righteousness. However, no where does he tell us that He will serve us in bed, if were perfectly normal and able to get up. If we can work, we must, and thus eat. So, I'm trusting God with this situation. However, I want to do what I can to beat this cancer, just as I would work to earn money for bread that God gives me to eat. Thank you for fighting with me and for me.

My sincere love to you all.

Robbie

You may contact Pastor Robbie Spencer at ...

Robbie Spencer
1195 Pitman Valley Road | Campbellsville, KY 42718
270-849-4192
spencer.robbie@gmail.com
FaceBook

SEPTEMBER 4, 2016 · WEEK 1

THE PEACEFUL KINGDOM

Bible Passage: Isaiah 11:1-9

Key Verse - Isaiah 11:9

They shall not hurt nor destroy in all my holy mountain: for the earth shall be full of the knowledge of the Lord, as the waters cover the sea

Introduction and Background

Rahab, a harlot of Jericho, whom the Bible tells us hid two Hebrew spies that Joshua sent to spy out the land, helped the two spies to escape *(Joshua 2:1-21)* This Rahab became an ancestor of David, the king, and of Jesus, the Messiah; *(Joshua 6:17-25; Matthew 1:5)*. Rahab's house was on the city wall of Jericho. Rahab also manufactured and dyed linen. She secretly housed the two spies whom Joshua sent to explore Jericho and helped them escape by hiding them in the piles of flax stalks on her roof-top. She used these products in her cloth and dyeing business *(Joshua 2:6)*. Rahab sent the king's messengers on a false trail, and then let the two spies down the outside wall by a rope through the window of her house *(Joshua 2:15)*.

When the Israelites captured Jericho, they spared the house with the scarlet cord in the window, which was a sign that a friend of God's people lived in that house. Therefore Rahab, along with her father and mother, her brothers, and all her father's household, were spared. Apparently she and her family were later brought into the nation of Israel because Matthew refers to Rahab as the wife of Salmon **(SAL** munn – Ruth 4:20-21; Matthew 1:4-5; Luke 3:32; 1 Chronicles 2:11). Salmon was the son of Nahshon *(NAH shun)* - a son of Amminadab (a **MEN** uh dab – 1 Chronicles 2:9-12). Nahshon was a prince and leader among the tribes of Judah during the wilderness wanderings *(Numbers 2:3)*, and a descendant of the great house of Pharez *(FAR ease)*, through Hezron (**HEZ** ron). Nahshon was the father of Salmon who married Rahab and they became the parents of Boaz (**BOW** ahz). Their son Boaz married Ruth, the Moabitess, and they became the parents of Obed (**OH** bed). Obed was the father of Jesse and Jesse was the father of David the king. Thus Ruth, a Moabitess, and Rahab, a Canaanite harlot, became part of the lineage of King David out of which the Messiah would come *(Matthew 1:5)*. Here God gives us an early insight into God's grace and forgiveness extended to all, not limited by nationality, nor by gender or by the nature of a person's sins.

The Scriptures do not tell us how Rahab, who came out of a culture where harlotry and idolatry were acceptable, recognized Jehovah as the ONE and ONLY true God, but her insights recorded in Joshua 2:9-11 leave no doubt that she did so. Thus a Canaanite woman's declaration of faith led the writer of the Epistle to the Hebrews to cite Rahab as one of the heroes of faith *(Hebrews 11:31)*, while James commended her as an example of one who has been justified by faithful works *(James 2:25)*.

Jesse's designation as "the **Ephrathite** (***EF*** ruh thite) of Bethlehem Judah" *(1 Samuel 17:12)* implies that Jesse was one of the very old families in the house of Judah. Jesse was the father of eight sons — Eliab (e ***LIE*** ab), Abinadab (uh ***BIN*** uh dab), Shimea (***SHIM*** ee ah), Nethanel (nih ***THAN*** ee al), Raddai (***RAD*** eye), Ozem (***OH*** zim), Elihu (e ***LIE*** hue), and King David, who was his youngest son. There were also two daughters, Zeruiah (zeh roo EYE ah) and Abigail (***AB*** ih gail). The title "**son of Jesse**" soon became attached to David. It was sometimes used in a spirit of insult and ridicule, mocking David's humble shepherd origins *(1 Samuel 20:27; 1 Kings 12:16)*. Shepherds were considered at the bottom of the social strata in Jewish society.

While considered low on the social structure of the Jews, Jesse was high on the financial structure. His head for his shepherding business had been blessed of God and parlayed into a very profitable and lucrative business for the house of Jesse. The prophet Isaiah spoke of "**a Rod from the stem of Jesse**" *(Isaiah 11:1)* and of *"a Root of Jesse" (Isaiah11:10)*. Other prophecies of the Messiah to come are from the apostle Paul and the prophets Jeremiah and Zechariah with "a branch" *(Jeremiah 23:5 and Zechariah 3:8)* and a "root of Jesse" *(Romans 15:12).*

In Isaiah's prophecies, the present and future get intermingled. In the previous chapter, Isaiah had represented the Assyrian king and his army under the image of a dense and flourishing forest, with all its glory and grandeur. This speaks of the then present Assyrian oppression and captivity. In chapter eleven, he contrasts this metaphor describing the personage whom he sees in the far-distant future as the image of a slender twig or shoot, sprouting up from the root of a decayed and fallen tree. Between the Assyrians, therefore, and the person who is the subject of this chapter, there is a most striking and beautiful contrast given. The one was like a thick expansive forest, which would soon fall and decay; the other was this little sprout from a decayed tree, which would rise and flourish.

Isaiah is filled with numerous prophecies of Jesus as the Messiah and Isaiah's use of the word "Branch" is significant. The Hebrew language has no uppercase letters, but the word is capitalized here in our modern Scripture account. This is to call attention to the Messianic inference of the **One** being foretold. For the prophets Jeremiah and Zechariah it was "a **Branch**" *(Jeremiah 23:5 and Zechariah 3:8).* The Hebrew word for "Branch" – *neetser* (**NAY'** tser– meaning a shoot or sprout) – will grow from the "Root" of Jesse. This may bring greater illumination to the passage in the New Testament Gospels, *(Matthew 2:23)* which states that Jesus resided in the town of Nazareth, "...that it might be fulfilled which was spoken by the prophets, He shall be called a Nazarene." There is a closeness in the sound of the words Nazareth and *neetzer (**NAY** tser)*. Perhaps Matthew had the "Branch" in mind as the fulfillment of Isaiah's prophecy in signifying this lowly village where Jesus grew up.

The Messiah Brings Real Hope
Isaiah 11:1-5

1 And there shall come forth a rod out of the stem of Jesse, and a Branch shall grow out of his roots:
2 And the spirit of the Lord shall rest upon him, the spirit of wisdom and understanding, the spirit of counsel and might, the spirit of knowledge and of the fear of the Lord;
3 And shall make him of quick understanding in the fear of the Lord: and he shall not judge after the sight of his eyes, neither reprove after the hearing of his ears:
4 But with righteousness shall he judge the poor, and reprove with equity for the meek of the earth: and he shall smite the earth with the rod of his mouth, and with the breath of his lips shall he slay the wicked.
5 And righteousness shall be the girdle of his loins, and faithfulness the girdle of his reins.

Isaiah predicts that the Messiah would come in the midst of a seemingly hopeless situation. However, our great God specializes in bringing hope out of hopelessness! Using this metaphor, the prophet of God begins his communication of God's new plan of redemption and reconciliation to reconcile fallen men and fallen nations back to Him. Though it would take years for it to unfold, God uses Isaiah to open the prophetic door upon this divine revelation and to slowly reveal the "**Redeemer**" Who was still far, far out in the tomorrow of time.

"**And a branch**"... **(neetser):** (v.1) a twig, branch, or shoot; a slip or young sucker of a tree, that is selected for transplanting, requiring it to be watched with special care as it develops. The fact that this "**root**" is expressly applied to Jesus in the New Testament by the Apostle Paul in Romans 15:12 as applicable to the times of the Messiah is further authentication of what the ancient prophet Isaiah was seeing as a dim glimpse of the coming Messiah. Isaiah saw Him coming while Paul saw Him as having arrived. Isaiah uses these opening verses and the metaphors therein to communicate the new plan that God is unfolding.

The spirit of the Lord resting upon him is a reference to the very breath of God. Using the Hebrew word meaning one's very breath, the divine *ruakh* (**RUE akh**) of God, would rest upon the Messiah. John in the Revelation of Jesus Christ speaks: "**...and there were seven lamps of fire burning before the throne, which** are the seven Spirits of God" *(Revelation 4:5)*. Notice that Spirits is in upper case! Again: "....and seven eyes, which are the seven Spirits of God sent forth into all the earth" *(Revelation 5:6)*. Lamps are for light and eyes are to let light in and seven is the number of fullness. These symbols speak of the fullness of the Holy Spirit of God resting upon the prophesied Messiah. Reading Isaiah 11:2 we have there the *Spirit of the Lord* (1), the *wisdom of the Lord* (2), *the understanding of the Lord* (3), the counsel of the Lord (4), *the might of the Lord* (5), *the knowledge of the Lord* (6), and *the reverence* (fear or understanding) *of the Lord* (7) — that is all there is and all that the Holy Spirit is in the person and presence of the third person of the God-head. Indeed, when the Holy Spirit descended from heaven and rested bodily upon the Son, Jesus Christ, as He was baptized by John in the waters of the Jordan, and the voice of the Father saying. "This is my beloved Son, in whom I am well pleased" *(Matthew 3:17)*, the fullness of the Lord came upon God's Christ to empower Him to carry out His Father's mission on earth and Jesus' public ministry was launched. The Gospel of the Kingdom and the Holy Spirit of God were sent forth into all the earth *(Revelation 5:6)*. All of the attributes of righteousness, justice, reverence, respect, equity and faithfulness were embodied in Jesus, the Son of God and the Messiah.

Ponder Points

How important is it that we take steps to ensure that

the church's plans, programs, and projects fall in line and harmony with the work of the Branch (Jesus)? How about individuals, should they not be on the same page? How can we be models of the attributes of the Messiah and of the Holy Spirit in regard to judgment and righteousness?

The Messiah Gives True Peace
Isaiah 11:6-9

6 The wolf also shall dwell with the lamb, and the leopard shall lie down with the kid; and the calf and the young lion and the fatling together; and a little child shall lead them.

7 And the cow and the bear shall feed; their young ones shall lie down together: and the lion shall eat straw like the ox.

8 And the sucking child shall play on the hole of the asp, and the weaned child shall put his hand on the cockatrice' den.

9 They shall not hurt nor destroy in all my holy mountain: for the earth shall be full of the knowledge of the Lord, as the waters cover the sea.

Many people tell us that this passage is speaking of a great era of peace on this earth which will last for one thousand years. We are told that all war shall cease, all crime will be suspended and all disease will be conquered while people live with an abundance of comfort and peace in the midst of unparalleled bliss and longevity. Even the animals will be totally tame and peacefully abide together in a utopia of peace and tranquility. When asked what they base these claims on, they confidently refer to this passage and others in Isaiah as proof texts for their belief in a millennial reign of Christ and accept literally what Isaiah says is promised by God in these verses.

The question to consider and resolve is whether Isaiah is describing the actual physical and literal condition of the world during a future 1000 year earthly reign of Christ, or whether his language is a figurative disclosure of the effect of the Gospel of the Kingdom during the present age? During this period of 1000 years, called a "millennium" derived from the compounding of the Latin "mille" (**MILL** lay – one thousand), and "annum" (**AWN** um – year), people will live to be hundreds of years old, death will be suspended and peace and plenty will be the order of the day. Most who hold this view also tell of the New Jerusalem coming down from God out of heaven with dimensions of fifteen hundred miles square and with walls fifteen hundred miles high. This literal interpretation of Scripture and all their predictions are predicated upon and begin with a literal application of Isaiah's prophecies.

Such an application of Isaiah's prophecies certainly opens a Pandora's Box of unsolvable questions. For example: At the present time the population of the world is doubling every 15 to 20 years, If we were to begin with our present population of 7.4 billion people and if we did not exceed our present rate of increase, a very conservative estimate of the world's population in 1000 years would be that number would be 4.3 **septillion** people. That number would look like this, 4,300, with eighteen more zeros behind it — 4,300,000,000,000,000,000,000. We are assured that the mortality rate during this millennium will be practically nil while the birth rate will spiral much higher. Just plain arithmetic tells us that this planet could not sustain such numbers.

And if you think the problem created by human population is staggering, just add to it what the unimpeded proliferation of the animals will mean. I cannot begin to fathom the population of the rabbits and rats, along with the reptiles and bats in 1,000 years of no death and dying. We are told that the lion will no longer be carnivorous, but will eat straw along with the ox. So will all other carnivores. Even man himself will have to be 100% vegetarian when it comes to food. How could the earth produce enough vegetation to feed the teeming multitudes of animals, let alone the unimaginable multitudes of human-kind? How can the preachers make it without fried chicken?

It is apparent that a literal application and interpretation of this passage does create some staggering and unanswerable dilemmas. Let us find the answer by comparing Scripture with Scripture. Let us test a figurative or symbolic interpretation in the light of God's Word. There are approximately 140 references to lions and lionesses in the Bible according to Young's

Analytical Concordance. Many are figurative as this one from Zephaniah (zeff ah *NYE* ah): "Her princes within her ARE roaring lions; her judges ARE evening wolves; they gnaw not the bones till the morrow" *(Zephaniah 3:3 – KJV)*. Other places where animals characterize people are Genesis 49:9, 14, 17, 21 and Psalms 22:20-21; 35:17; 58:4-6, just to cite a few. Even Jesus scathingly denounced the scribes and Pharisees calling them a generation of serpents and vipers *(Matthew 23:33)*. Remember when Sister Lillie S. McCutchcon made this same point in her preaching where Jesus called Herod a fox in Luke 13:32? We can multiply text upon text to validate a figurative interpretation and application is intended here.

Others concur. The Standard Lesson Commentary states, "The other potential interpretation is to see the prophecies fulfilled in a more figurative sense, with the animals representing humans who clash with one another. In the Bible, human enemies are often compared with animals (Psalm 22:12, 13, 16, 20, 21; Acts 20:29; etc.). But because of the Branch's impact and the forgiveness and peace He brings about (through Jesus' death and resurrection), hatred and bitterness are no more." Salvation and sanctification change our nature. A lamb truly can be safe with a lion when their natures have been changed.

Let me close our comments on this passage with this little poem that says it all very well:

— Millennial Musings —

"Come," said the Lion to the Lamb,*"*
Come into my fold,
And let's lie down together as it's been foretold."
"Oh, no, no", said the Lamb to the Lion,
"That cannot be true, I read that in God's Word,
but it doesn't mean **ME** *and* **YOU***!*
"Jesus did not come to change our animal nature.
It is **MAN** *who needs help to become a '*
NEW CREATURE*'!" "I never thought of it that away"*
said the Lion, *"And what you*
Say could be true — I know I have a strong desire
For mutton and really don't think straw will do!
But there's one thing that puzzles me
and I can't quite understand!
If we as 'dumb animals' *can figure this out,*
WHY CAN'T MAN?*"*

(Unknown)

Ponder Points

What can your church do to help a fallen world to move toward the ideal picture painted by Isaiah in our Scripture lesson? What can you as an individual do in *'out-reach'* [Evangelism] to share the Gospel, do in *'in-reach'* [Sanctification] within your own being, life, and living, and in *'up-reach'* [Worship] in your individual devotions, worship, praise and adoration?

Conclusion

Peaceful isn't a word that would describe our time or culture. Instead crises, chaos, unrest, turmoil, hatred, strife, confrontations, war, murder, fear and terrorism are more accurate descriptive words that would fit our present world. While a great many are looking for our Lord to bring an earthly time of world peace and tranquility of a thousand years duration, and a time of great revival and return of the masses to Jesus Christ, it was Jesus who asked the question "...**Nevertheless when the Son of man cometh, shall he find faith on the earth**" *(Luke 18:6-8)*? Paul cautioned young Timothy with the charge: "**But evil men and seducers shall wax worse and worse, deceiving, and being deceived**" *(2 Timothy 3:13)*. It is the character of fallen men to do this and this is no surprise. This is the general *law of depravity* — that of an un-converted human-kind. They are always going to grow worse, sinking into iniquity more and more. The caution here to Timothy was not to expect any exemption from persecution *(2 Timothy 3:12)*. He was to anticipate such. He was to regard it as certain that he, as well as others, would be persecuted. In the face of that which was certain, Paul instructed him to "**Preach the word; be instant in season, out of season; reprove, rebuke, exhort with all longsuffering and doctrine**" *(2 Timothy 4:2)*. He was warned that his hearers would not want to hear it and would reject it and him; but, he was to persevere and in doing so save his own soul and those who would hear and heed.

This same instruction is current and most applicable to our present juncture in this time world. Jesus is the final answer, but He is not coming to set up an earthly, literal kingdom on this terrestrial ball we call earth nor in this time world! When He comes again, He is coming as **KING** of kings and **LORD** of lords not to set up a kingdom here, but to "gather up" a kingdom from this world, the one which He established at His First Coming. Jesus said in Luke 16:16, "The law and prophets were until John: since that time the kingdom of God is preached, and every man presseth into it." Who are the "kings and lords (priests)" in this kingdom? John tells us who they are in Revelation 1:6 and Revelation 5:10:

> "And hath made US kings and priests unto God and his Father; to him be glory and dominion for ever and ever. Amen" — "And hast made US unto our God kings and priests: and we shall reign on the earth"

The "kingdom" is here and NOW, a present reality, and the KING is coming to take it from earth to heaven. Until then the apostle Peter said:

> "Nevertheless we, according to his promise, look for new heavens and A NEW EARTH, wherein dwelleth righteousness" *(2 Peter 3:13)*, and Jesus said, "Occupy till I come" *(Luke 19:13).*

Barney E. Warren gave us a great song about this present Kingdom of God and the peace it brings:

The Kingdom of Peace

There's a theme that is sweet to my mem'ry,
There's a joy that I cannot express,
There's a treasure that gladdens my being,
'Tis the kingdom of God's righteousness.

There's a scene of its grandness before me,
Of its greatness there can be no end;
It is joy, it is peace, it is glory,
In my heart, how these riches do blend!

I am lost in its splendor and beauty,
To its ne'er-fading heights I would rise,
Till I see the King come to receive me,
And explore it with Him in the skies.

What a pleasure in life it is bringing!
What assurance and hope ever bright!
O what rapture and bliss are awaiting,
When our faith shall be lost in the sight!

'Tis a kingdom of peace, it is reigning within,
It shall ever increase in my soul;
We possess it right here when He saves from all sin,
And 'twill last while the ages shall roll.

-*Worship the Lord: Hymnal of the Church of God*
(Anderson, IN: Warner Press, 1989), 481.

The circumstances of many Christians are stormy. Many face anguish because of family problems. Some face addictions. Some live in war zones like Syria where the last children's hospital in the City of Aleppo was bombed. Refugees by the millions cross borders. Jesus was clear: "In the world ye shall have tribulation" (John 16:33b). But He also said, "But be of good cheer; I have overcome the world" (16:33c) and "These things I have spoken unto you, that in me ye might have peace" (16:33a). Thank God for the spiritual, present Kingdom of Peace!

Prayer

Father, we thank you for the present Kingdom of God within us. In all the storms of life, we can look to you to sustain peace. May we allow you to change our natures that we can live in peace with all.

Parting Thought
Contentment with the divine
will is the best medicine for daily living!

Vocabulary

Metaphor: Something used to represent something else.

Millennium: A period of 1000 years.

Parlay: To use one's money, talents, assets to achieve wealth and success.

Utopia: An ideal place or state.

SEPTEMBER 11, 2016 · WEEK 2

THE MOUNTAIN OF GOD

Bible Passage: Isaiah 25:6-10

Key Verse - Isaiah 25:8

He will swallow up death in victory; and the Lord God will wipe away tears from off all faces; and the rebuke of his people shall he take away from off all the earth: for the Lord hath spoken it.

Introduction and Bible Background

Many mountains are mentioned in the Bible, including Mounts Horeb (*HOHR* ebb), Gerizim (geh *RUH* zim), Ebal (*EE* bull), Nebo (*NEE* bow), Pisgah (*PIZ* gah), Carmel (*KAHR* muhl), Hermon (*HUR* mon). God uses mountains as the backdrop for great things and great truths.

— The ark came to rest on the mountains of Ararat (*AIR* uh rat):

Genesis 8:4
And the ark rested in the seventh month, on the seventeenth day of the month, upon the mountains of Ararat.

- The Law was given on Mount Sinai (**SIGH** knee eye):
  Exodus 34:29

  And it came to pass, when Moses came down from mount Sinai with the two tables of testimony in Moses' hand, when he came down from the mount, that Moses wist not that the skin of his face shone while he talked with him.

- Mount of Transfiguration
  Mark 9:

  2 And after six days Jesus taketh with him Peter, and James, and John, and leadeth them up into an high mountain apart by themselves: and he was transfigured before them.

  3 And his raiment became shining, exceeding white as snow; so as no fuller on earth can white them.

  4 And there appeared unto them Elias with Moses: and they were talking with Jesus.

- The mountain of the Lord's house (The coming kingdom and the church):

  Isaiah 2:1-2
  1 The word that Isaiah the son of Amoz saw concerning Judah and Jerusalem.
  2 And it shall come to pass in the last days, that the mountain of the Lord's house shall be established in the top of the mountains, and shall be exalted

above the hills; and all nations shall flow unto it.
— Fulfillment:

Hebrews 1:
1 God, who at sundry times and in divers manners spake in time past unto the fathers by the prophets,
2 Hath in these last days spoken unto us by his Son, whom he hath appointed heir of all things, by whom also he made the worlds;
3 Who being the brightness of his glory, and the express image of his person, and upholding all things by the word of his power, when he had by himself purged our sins, sat down on the right hand of the Majesty on high;

Hebrews 12:
22 **But ye are come unto mount Sion**, and unto the city of the living God, the heavenly Jerusalem, and to an innumerable company of angels,
23 **To the general assembly and church of the firstborn**, which are written in heaven, and to God the Judge of all, and to the spirits of just men made perfect,
24 And to Jesus the mediator of the new covenant, and to the blood of sprinkling, that speaketh better things than that of Abel.

— The church on a great and HIGH mountain:

Revelation 21:

1 And I saw a new heaven and a new earth: for the first heaven and the first earth were passed away; and there was no more sea.
2 And I John saw the holy city, new Jerusalem, coming down from God out of heaven, prepared as a bride adorned for her husband.
Revelation 21:9-10 And there came unto me one of the seven angels which had the seven vials full of the seven last plagues, and talked with me, saying, Come hither, I will shew thee the bride, the Lamb's wife. And he carried me away in the spirit to a great and high mountain and shewed me that great city, the holy Jerusalem, descending out of heaven from God.

Throughout the whole of Isaiah the prophet describes God as sitting high yet looking low. This is an image of God being elevated above His creation. In Isaiah 2:2 the prophets speak of the last days when the mountain of the LORD's house shall be established in the tops of the mountains. This is a reference to the coming Messiah and His kingdom when His church will be elevated above all of the systems (**mountains**) of men. While God's place is above creation, that does not cause Him to forget His creation. He is above creation, but He chooses to be involved in creation — above, yet still in. Our lesson today is a vivid portrayal of God being involved. It is a picture of God protecting, providing and promoting a people who will be His people. Leading up to today's text, chapter 24 of Isaiah gives details of God's judgment of the wicked. It pictures the whole earth laid waste *(Isaiah 24:1-13)*. The final verses *(vv. 17-23)* depict God rounding up the enemies of His people as prisoners. Isaiah 25 shifts the focus opening with a song of praise for the way judgment has vindicated the faith God's remnant have placed in Him.

A Wonderful Feast
Isaiah 25:6-8

6   And in this mountain shall the Lord of hosts make unto all people a feast of fat things, a feast of wines on the lees, of fat things full of marrow, of wines on the lees well refined.
7   And he will destroy in this mountain the face of the covering cast over all people, and the vail that is spread over all nations.
8   He will swallow up death in victory; and the Lord God will wipe away tears from off all faces; and the rebuke of his people shall he take away from off all the earth: for the Lord hath spoken it. KJV

It is interesting to note that the sovereign Lord does not limit this feast just to Judah, but rather this feast is for all people. Why is that? God as we are explicitly told in the New Testament, is no respecter of persons — Jew or Gentile. The offer of salvation is open to "**whosoever believeth**" (John 3:16). This includes everyone! God does not glory in the destruction of the wicked. If judgment and destruction cannot be avoided in the end in the name of righteous justice, punishment is not what God ultimately wants to do. Rather, He wants to invite "**all peoples (whosoever will)**" to His feast *(Isaiah 15:6)*. The word "all" is not accidental, for it is repeated four more times in verses 7 and 8. Isaiah is telling us clearly that everyone on earth is invited to this celebration!

Notice also that verse 8 talks about God removing this "shroud" that hangs over all mankind. This is the specter of death. With this cloud of gloom removed from over His people, they can see the bigger picture. When Jesus rose from the tomb, death had been conquered! Paul tells us in the Corinthian letter *(1 Corinthians 15:26-28)* that the last enemy is death and Christ has vanquished that specter for all time by His resurrection from the dead.

1 Corinthians 15:54-55

54 So when this corruptible shall have put on incorruption, and this mortal shall have put on immortality, then shall be brought to pass the saying that is written, Death is swallowed up in victory.

55 O death, where is thy sting? O grave, where is thy victory? KJV

Through Jesus Christ, God's only Son, and our Redeemer, God has completely removed this "shroud" for all who reside on and in His mountain. Men risk their lives to scale the great and majestic mountains of the world just to stand on their summits. But all of those mountain pale and fade into insignificance compared to the Mount of Calvary. There, instead of us risking our life to enjoy what God has on top of His mountain, Jesus gave His life for us so that we could enjoy the feast God has prepared for us at the summit of His mountain. This Feast is called the Marriage Supper of the Lamb *(Revelation 19:9).*

Ponder Points

Do you think *"mountaintop experiences"* are important? What are some ways you can create such experiences in your worship services and the social gatherings of the people of the church? Can clear, open and honest proclamation of the Word in teaching and preaching be beneficial in creating such happenings?

Wonderful Trust
Isaiah 25:9-10

9   And it shall be said in that day, Lo, this is our God; we have waited for him, and he will save us: this is the Lord; we have waited for him, we will be glad and rejoice in his salvation.
10 For in this mountain shall the hand of the Lord rest, and Moab shall be trodden down under him, even as straw is trodden down for the dunghill. KJV

Isaiah 25 began with Isaiah's personal tribute of praise, "O Lord, thou art my God; I will exalt thee, I will praise thy name" *(v. 1)*. The praise has now extended to the lips of all who will come to the mountain of the Lord to share in all the "wonderful things" provided there *(v. 1)*. The feast and the good thing result from the acknowledgment of God as a mighty Savior. On this day, finally, God's sovereignty, love, protection and provision will be fully recognized by all. Just as the ancient remnant worshipers waited for the coming Messiah, now all, Jew and Gentile alike, who recognize Jesus Christ as Lord and Savior are looking for His return. They have ceased to place their trust in any other than Jesus as Lord.

Across Scripture God is depicted as a protector of His people. There are verses in our passage where that protection is mirrored: God is "**a strength to the poor, a strength to the needy .... a refuge from the storm, a shadow from the heat**" *(Isaiah 25:4)*. Our text *(v.9)* says that "**he will save us**".

Our God is a God of power, a God of deliverance, and a God of protection. He is the Alpha and the Omega, the Beginning and the End, the First and the Last. He is our ALL in ALL and His protection and love will never end.

But now we come to verse 10. There we see portrayed the hand of the Lord that has been active throughout Scripture as being at rest. God will rest after He ushers in His new heaven and new earth. Before that rest the "**last enemy**" *(1 Corinthians 15:26)* which is death will be destroyed. At the return of Jesus Christ, death, along with all whose names are not in the Book of Life, shall be cast into the Lake of Fire (**Revelation 20:14-15**) never again to cause heartache, pain and tears.

However the closing portion of that verse depicts something very different from the joy and celebration that has been portrayed in the preceding verses. Here is the conclusion in its entirety which actually extends down into verses 11-12: "**The Moabites shall be trodden down in their place as straw is trodden down in the dung-pit. Even though they spread out their hands as swimmers spread their hands to swim, their pride will be laid low despite the struggle of their hands. All their strong towers and fortresses will be brought down.**"

The final point must be made that while God is merciful and compassionate, slow to anger and quick to forgive, still no one should dare to presume upon His grace and compassion! For someone to live a sinful life, thinking that God will not notice is utter foolishness. Sin will ultimately be punished and that means there will absolutely not be any exception to that deadly consequence. The end of time will be marked with a great gathering and celebration of ALL of God's children where all will be blessed. What a day that will be! But, it will also be marked by a terrible destruction on those who refused to turn to God in their trust, trusting in their own fortresses (**methods and mountains** – *denominations and religions*) to save them.

Conclusion

One could not close today's lesson without remembering that tragic day in our nation's history. On September 11th, 2001 2,977 victims lost their lives in that terrorists attack upon the twin Trade Towers in New York City. Yet death goes right on claiming over 7000 people every day in these United States of America. People are dealing on every hand with death, planning funeral services, visiting grave sites, struggling to sort through belongings and affairs of departed family members. Death is never a welcome visitor. People put their trust in government to protect them, in the economy to protect them, in their IRA's and financial nest eggs to provide for them.

The early church of God certainly knew oppression. John tells us that a great red dragon faced the newborn church of God in Rev. 12 and had to flee into the wilderness to a place prepared by God. When John looks at the outcome, the end of the match, he sees the church with the Lord on Mt. Zion! "And I looked, and, lo, a Lamb stood on the mount Sion and with him an hundred forty and four thousand, having his Father's name written in their foreheads" (Rev. 14:1). John saw the church victorious on the mount Sion with the Lamb! When Stephen was stoned, he saw Jesus standing. When the church was confronted by the enemy, John saw Jesus standing. Whatever oppression and depression you face today in your life, Jesus cares. You are His attention. He stands for you. Find Him on His mountain.

Brother O.L. Johnson changed a little two-lettered word one year at Pastors' Fellowship from "to" to "in" as we sang *We're Marching in Zion:*

> Come, we that love the Lord,
> And let our joys be known;
> Join in a song with sweet accord,
> And thus surround the throne.
>
>> Refrain:
>> We're marching *in* Zion,
>> Beautiful, beautiful Zion;
>> We're marching upward *in* Zion,
>> The beautiful city of God.
>
> The sorrows of the mind
> Be banished from the place;
> Religion never was designed
> To make our pleasures less.
>
>> Let those refuse to sing,
>> Who never knew our God;
>> But children of the heav'nly King
>> May speak their joys abroad.
>
> The men of grace have found
> Glory begun below;
> Celestial fruits on earthly ground
> From faith and hope may grow.
>
>> The hill of Zion yields
>> A thousand sacred sweets

Before we reach the heav'nly fields,
Or walk the golden streets.

Then let our songs abound,
And every tear be dry;
We're marching through Immanuel's ground
To fairer worlds on high.

Today's lesson tells us to put our hope in the Lord and His mountain (**the kingdom of God – *Matthew 6:33***), where all their aspirations will be fulfilled. The violence and oppression, and death that plagues us every waking hour will one day be destroyed and eternity will unfold before us as we gather on God's holy mountain. Until then Isaiah 40: 29 – 31 tells us to "**wait**" and "**hope**". If you are not willing to wait while trusting in the Lord, you will never experience the joy of knowing that it is the Lord who brought you through it all, kept you, and saved you. We must continue to wait on God until that day becomes reality. Be of good courage and "**Wait**"!

Prayer

Our Heavenly Father, help us not to miss the feast you have prepared. You have invited us to the marriage supper of the Lamb and we sure don't want to miss it. Help us to climb Mt. Zion to be with you in hope and victory. Amen.

Parting Thought

When discouraged, think of the mountain!

Isaiah 40:31
But they that wait upon the Lord
shall renew their strength;
they shall mount up with wings as eagles;
they shall run, and not be weary;
and they shall walk, and not faint.
KJV

SEPTEMBER 18, 2016 · WEEK 3

FOUNDATIONS OF THE EARTH

Bible Passage: Isaiah 40:21 – 31

Key Verse - Isaiah 40:28
Hast thou not known? hast thou not heard, that the everlasting God, the Lord, the Creator of the ends of the earth, fainteth not, neither is weary? there is no searching of his understanding.
KJV

Introduction and Background

As has been often stated, the book of Isaiah is typically divided into two sections by commentators. The first section, chapters one through thirty-nine, is filled with warnings to Israel and Judah of impending destruction due to their disobedience. Israel and Judah' judgment certainly is foreshadowed, but also judgment upon the nations around them. Assyria, which had been their nemesis for so long, was no longer a threat to God's people. Babylon is the new heavy on the block. Isaiah 40 is a significant turning point in the book of Isaiah. Up to this point, the prophetic oracles have largely been about impending judgment on Judah and the surrounding nations of that day. Judah worshiped idols and committed oppression; as a result they will be judged with other nations. This judgment will result in exile, and the people of God will be scattered to the ends of the earth. The second half of the book, chapters forty through sixty-six, looks ahead to the time when God's people are in Babylonian captivity. According to Jeremiah 25:9-11, God's people were in captivity in Babylon seventy years. Isaiah, as just mentioned, was written in anticipation of that, during a time when Israel and Judah were prospering. Because they did not heed the warnings of God's Word through the prophets in the midst of their prosperity, they found themselves captives in a strange land. As Creator, God cannot be controlled by any living person or thing that is under Him. He is not held captive by the desires and will of humanity. God is sovereign! Recalling this truth can be a comfort to people under oppression because it gives them proper perspective of their predicament.

Today's text brings comfort to the people in exile, reminding them that God is still in control and there is none like Him. The prophet Isaiah, in Isa. 40:22, encourages the people to remember that God is sovereign and is in control.

God's Power Over Creation
Isaiah 40:21-22

21 Have ye not known? have ye not heard? hath it

not been told you from the beginning? have ye not understood from the foundations of the earth?

22 It is he that sitteth upon the circle of the earth, and the inhabitants thereof are as grasshoppers; that stretcheth out the heavens as a curtain, and spreadeth them out as a tent to dwell in: KJV

While yet people thought that the world was flat, and thousands of years before they found out that it was round, Isaiah intimated the shape of it. The most beautiful figure in all geometry is the circle. God made the universe on the plan of a circle. In the natural world there are straight lines, angles, parallelograms, diagonals, quadrangles; but these evidently are not God's favorites. Out of a great many figures God seems to have selected the circle as the best. "It is He that sitteth upon the circle of the earth." The stars are in a circle (orbit), the moon is in a circle (orbit), the sun is in a circle (orbit), the universe in a circle (orbit), and the throne of God is the center of that circle (orbit). The history of the world goes in a circle.

What is true in the material universe is true in God's moral government and spiritual arrangement. That is the meaning of Ezekiel's wheel; the wheel means God's providence. But a wheel is of no use unless it turns around, and if it turns around it moves in a circle. Bad or good actions may make the circuit of many years, but come back to us they will, as certainly as that God sits on the circle of the earth. The "preacher" of Ecclesiastes said, Ecclesiastes 11:1 "Cast thy bread upon the waters:

for thou shalt find it after many days" *KJV.* It will come full-circle.

God's Power Over Human Authority
Isaiah 40:23-27

23 That bringeth the princes to nothing; he maketh the judges of the earth as vanity.
24 Yea, they shall not be planted; yea, they shall not be sown: yea, their stock shall not take root in the earth: and he shall also blow upon them, and they shall wither, and the whirlwind shall take them away as stubble.
25 To whom then will ye liken me, or shall I be equal? saith the Holy One.
26 Lift up your eyes on high, and behold who hath created these things, that bringeth out their host by number: he calleth them all by names by the greatness of his might, for that he is strong in power; not one faileth.
27 Why sayest thou, O Jacob, and speakest, O Israel, My way is hid from the Lord, and my judgment is passed over from my God? KJV

All princes and kings *(v. 23),* no matter how great their power, their wealth, and their dignity, they are, by His hand, reduced to nothing before Him. The design of this passage *(v.23)* is to contrast the majesty of God with that of princes and nobles, and to show how far He excels them all. The general truth is therefore stated, that all monarchs are by Him removed from their thrones, and consigned to nothing. The idea in this verse *(v.24)* is that their name and family should become extinct in the same way as a tree does from which no shoot or sprout springs up. Although they were great and mighty, like the tree that sends out far-spreading branches, and strikes its roots deep, yet God would so utterly destroy them that they should have no posterity, and their family become extinct.

In verse 25, Isaiah refers to God as "**Holy One**." There is no definite article found here so it would seem that Isaiah was using this phrase "**Holy One**" as a title or name for the Creator. The next verse *(v.26)* refers to the host of the cosmic and stellar heavenly bodies that one sees when they lift their eyes to the stars and Isaiah attributes their being and order to this "**Holy One**." He was making the comparison of what is finite man in compared to the marvelous structure and working of the cosmos? All that you see and all that there is has it beginning and is anchored in this "**Holy One**" who spoke it all into existence. Who can be compared with God?

Ponder Points

Based on your own experiences with God, what adjectives would you use to describe Him? When we see ourselves before this Sovereign of the Universe as but grasshoppers, how can we begin to appreciate our littleness and insignificance when compared with

God and His creation? Why is it important that we see ourselves as we are?

God's Power Over Our Lives
Isaiah 40:28-31

28 Hast thou not known? hast thou not heard, that the everlasting God, the Lord, the Creator of the ends of the earth, fainteth not, neither is weary? there is no searching of his understanding.

29 He giveth power to the faint; and to them that have no might he increaseth strength.

30 Even the youths shall faint and be weary, and the young men shall utterly fall:

31 But they that wait upon the Lord shall renew their strength; they shall mount up with wings as eagles; they shall run, and not be weary; and they shall walk, and not faint. KJV

This portion of Scripture is one that if often quoted and is one of the favorites of numberless saints who rest upon its provocative and powerful promises. Essentially, the foundation that we enjoy as God's children is not based on our place or standing in society, nor our obedience to governmental entities, nor even upon our own contributive efforts toward His work. God alone is our foundation, providing our protection on Himself alone. God's strength is the source of our strength. Isaiah repeats the question he first asked in verse 21, "**Have you not known? Have you not heard?** The Lord is the everlasting God, and He is the Creator of the ends of the earth. He does not faint, He does not grow weary, His understanding is limitlessness" *(v.28)* ?

Isaiah is saying, *"Has it not been preached, have you not heard as a crier would go through the streets proclaiming that the everlasting God has come to help His people? He is not limited and His power and strength will not fail or falter. The strongest of men, even the youthful whose stamina seems inexhaustible will faint and grow weary and weak, but our God, the Creator of the cosmos is never weary or weak. He offers sustaining power to those who wait for Him to renew their strength, they will mount up on the wings of the eagle and soar. They shall walk and not grow weary nor faint."* The prophet encourages the people to remember their God. God is not just sovereign; God does not just have power. His compassion does not run out because of our frailties. His people were in captivity, but He is willing to reverse their situation, just as the prophet Isaiah encourages the ancient people of God to remember their God, the good news is that God remembers us. Just as the thief at Calvary declared, "**Lord remember me**," all who have cried that same cry since have the assurance of a God that will remember them!

Conclusion

"Everlasting" (Hebrew *'olam*, (oh-**LOM**) means existing beyond the realm of time, as before time began, and without any end. Men only understand history in terms of a time-line, but the everlasting God sees everything without the blurring of time-lines. That is why our trust is well placed when placed in the "**everlasting God**". Our futures are assured in Him. He knows the past and all that has happened throughout all of time and He sees the future as man knows and views the past. He is at the helm of all the ages yet to come and will be there when the ages cease to be and time is no more.

Therefore, Isaiah shows us that God is greater than our finite minds can comprehend. He cares for mankind and though we are limited in our being, He has no limits. When we are emotionally drained, burnt out, hurt, and physically used up and exhausted, God is there to pick us up and carry us on His "**eagle's wings**". Think of young parents with little ones that rob them of their sleep and rest with crying babies in the long night hours. Think of the elderly couple who are becoming unable to care for one another. Those we depend upon for care cannot be depended on to forever pick us up when we fall down, because they, themselves have their physical limits and grow weary. But our God never slumbers nor sleeps *(Psalms 121:3-4)*. Isaiah 40 speaks comfort (peace) in the midst of turmoil. While our lives, as saints, may not be rife injustice and oppression on a daily basis, it is still comforting to know and to rest on hope in God and trust in His foundation that is our guarantee that under His watchful eye He will cause what might transpire in our lives to work toward our good and well-being. Our "waiting" is an act of faith put to the test.

Prayer

Dr. W. Dale Oldham, pastor of the large Park Place congregation in Anderson, Indiana, Christian Brotherhood Hour national radio ministry of the Church of God preacher, chairman of Warner Press board, busy evangelist, etc., would go to bed at night and cup his hands and place all of his cares, worries, problems, and prayers there. Then, he would lift up his hands to the Lord and say, "Lord, I've done the best I can do today. I'm tired now and need some rest. I give you all of these to take care of them for me." He then would fall fast asleep trusting God. Do you need some sleep?

Parting Thought

Let Martin Luther's hymn "A Mighty Fortress Is Our God" sum up today's lesson for us:

A mighty fortress is our God, a bulwark never failing;
Our helper He amid the flood of mortal ills prevailing.
For still our ancient foe, doth seek to work us woe;
His craft and power are great, and armed with cruel hate,
On earth is not his equal.
Did we in our own strength confide,
Our striving would be losing.
Were not the right Man on our side,
The Man of God's own choosing.

Dost ask who that may be? Christ Jesus, it is He;
Lord Sabaoth, His name, from age to age the same,
And He must win the battle.

SEPTEMBER 25, 2016 · WEEK 4

EVERLASTING COVENANT

Bible Passage: Isaiah 61:1- 4, 8- 10

Key Verse - Isaiah 61:8

I the Lord love judgment, I hate robbery for burnt offering; and I will direct their work in truth, and I will make an everlasting covenant with them.
KJV

Introduction and Background

Today's lesson is the final one in this unit of lessons on "The Sovereignty of the Father." This lesson, as have the others in this unit, has a Messianic delineation from the prophet Isaiah. It comes from one of last seven chapters, 60 through 66, which are filled with the growing hope of God's restoration of His people from Babylonian captivity. Here, as we saw last week, the predominant message is one of hope. Specifically, today's text reminds us of how God will see His everlasting covenant come to full fruition through the redemptive mission of the Messiah. Therefore, it is no surprise that Jesus Christ cites this passage in the sermon He delivered at the outset of His year of inauguration of public ministry. You find this in Luke's account of this event recorded in Luke 4:1, 17-19.

Eternal Promise
Isaiah 61:1-2

1 The Spirit of the Lord God is upon me; because the Lord hath anointed me to preach good tidings unto the meek; he hath sent me to bind up the brokenhearted, to proclaim liberty to the captives, and the opening of the prison to them that are bound;

2 To proclaim the acceptable year of the Lord, and the day of vengeance of our God; to comfort all that mourn; *KJV*

The speaker is not introduced by name. Therefore he may be the prophet Isaiah himself, or he may be the servant of Isaiah. But it is not really very important which, for the servant was representative of prophecy; and if it be the prophet who speaks here, he also speaks with the conscience of the whole function and aim of the prophetic order. Jesus Christ is the intended object and perfect fulfilment of the prophecy is non-debatable, the foreshadowing of Christ as the Servant Himself. The writer, with the trans-piercing gaze of the seer is more anxious to make clear in whom this ideal is realized; and through eyes of faith he sees the coming Messiah. That Jesus Christ of Nazareth so plainly fulfilled the vision, it becomes, indeed, a very minor question to ask whom the writer intended.

The acceptable year of the Lord (v.2) is an allusion to the year of Jubilee, when the trumpet was blown, and liberty was proclaimed throughout all the land *(Leviticus 25:9-10)*. In like manner the Messiah would come to proclaim universal liberty — liberty to the world from the degrading yoke of sin. The time of His coming would be a time when God would be pleased to proclaim through Him (Christ) universal emancipation from Satan's bondage, and to restore to fallen man the privilege of becoming the freedmen of the Lord.

Eternal Salvation

Isaiah 61:3 - 4

3 To appoint unto them that mourn in Zion, to give unto them beauty for ashes, the oil of joy for mourning, the garment of praise for the spirit of heaviness; that they might be called trees of righteousness, the planting of the Lord, that he might be glorified.
4 And they shall build the old wastes, they shall raise up the former desolations, and they shall repair the waste cities, the desolations of many generations.

How will God provide? In the ancient world when one was in deep pain, suffering loss or mourning over a lost loved one, this person laid aside their clothing and donned sackcloth and covered their head and body with ashes as a sign of their sorrow and deep mourning.

Today's text does not deny that. It agrees that there is a time for mourning. But then it encourages the people to get up and take off those ashes and re-dress themselves for deliverance and service when God is going to take them. Their ashes would be exchanged for the oil of gladness, and their mantle would be one of praise instead of a fainting spirit *(v.3)*. The world of living and just surviving are poles apart. Israel had been surviving in exile, but none were living the life they had hoped to live. Oppression and difficulty marked each day. But the Spirit began to stir and hints of change began to appear.

    Instead of a heavy, burdened, and oppressed spirit denoting those of a faint and desponding heart, reformation and restoration were ahead. These expressions are figurative, and are taken from the custom which prevailed more in Oriental countries and which is founded in the nature of expressing the emotions of the mind by the manner of apparel. They would be clothed with a Spirit of praise, blessed for they had mourned in and for Zion, the people of God. God has a purpose for those whom He blesses. They were empowered with a spirit of restoration. God gave them a new attitude about both their past and their present situations and through the prophet Isaiah even gave them a glimpse of the promised Messiah and His time on earth. Their future rested on how successful they would be in restoring and repairing their desolate land upon their return.

Ponder Points

What has God blessed you with to do for His kingdom work? Have you learned *"lessons"* from lost opportunities, past experiences which you could share or mentor to help equip others for kingdom work? What spiritual impact should we hope to share and contribute to those who come under our sphere of ministry and influence?

Eternal Covenant
Isaiah 61:8 -11

8 For I the Lord love judgment, I hate robbery for burnt offering; and I will direct their work in truth, and I will make an everlasting covenant with them.

9 And their seed shall be known among the Gentiles, and their offspring among the people: all that see them shall acknowledge them, that they are the seed which the Lord hath blessed.

10 I will greatly rejoice in the Lord, my soul shall be joyful in my God; for he hath clothed me with the garments of salvation, he hath covered me with the robe of righteousness, as a bridegroom decketh himself with ornaments, and as a bride adorneth herself with her jewels.

11 For as the earth bringeth forth her bud, and as the garden causeth the things that are sown in it to spring forth; so the Lord God will cause righteousness and praise to spring forth before all the nations. *KJV*

Our text resumes in verse eight with God's proclamation that He loves justice, and hates crookedness and robbery (v.8) declaring that He will not tolerate it. Instead He pledges to undergird and guide them in their work and efforts for Him. The Lord expects unreserved commitment from His people and anything less He sees as robbery. Now that they have returned home, they must present to the Lord offerings that are pleasing and acceptable to Him. Even though they had been unfaithful in the past, God pledges to them His faithfulness. Now Jesus Christ, as the Servant-Messiah, will help them to make room for the Gentiles.

In the final verses of today's text there is a marked shift. In verses 8 - 9, we saw God exulted in restoring His people to favor in His sight and reestablishing His covenant with them and the descendants of Abraham. In verse 10, the speaker says, "I will greatly rejoice in the Lord." Why? Because "He has clothed me with the garments of salvation, He has covered me with the robe of righteousness." These garments symbolize belief in the Lord as Savior and Redeemer. The righteousness herein mentioned and bestowed is not our own righteousness, for that is as "filthy rags" *(Isaiah 64:6)* before His holy eyes.

Isaiah 64:6

But we are all as an unclean thing, and all our righteousnesses are as filthy rags; and we all do fade as a leaf; and our iniquities, like the wind, have taken us away. *KJV*

This covenant, this covering, is made possible by God sending His Son, the Messiah, Jesus Christ, to be our Redeemer. The righteousness is only possible when one fully trusts in Jesus Christ as Lord and Savior. The "I" of verse ten no longer refers to God as the speaker here; someone else is now speaking. But who is it? I think it is the same One who is speaking in verse one **"The Spirit of the Lord God is upon me..."** What did Jesus say to the listeners in the synagogue in Nazareth when He launched into His public ministry? Luke 4:17 – 21 tells of Jesus reading today's text before that crowd. Having finished reading:

Luke 4:20-21

20 And he closed the book, and he gave it again to the minister, and sat down. And the eyes of all them that were in the synagogue were fastened on him.
21 And he began to say unto them, This day is this scripture fulfilled in your ears. *KJV*

Notice if you will that the imagery of verse 10 is very similar to that used to portray the church in the New Testament. There Christ is seen as the Bridegroom and the church as the bride. Isaiah gives us an unmistakable picture of the Lord Jesus Christ in this Old Testament prophecy. There is a tone of joy, the Anointed One is joyful because of the springing forth of salvation and righteousness. He exults because God has brought rejoicing and renewal to the land. It is pictured as the blossoming and springing up of flowers and fruits of a garden *(v.11)*. This joyous growth is to take place across the entire earth, so it is that salvation is available to any and all.

Conclusion

The bottom line is that God is Sovereign over the world in which we live. The deceiver would raise up a smoke screen and make you to believe that this is not so, but listen folks, Our God Reigns! If your life is filled with suffering and turmoil such as described in today's text, then it is time that your stir yourself, redress yourself, cast off the sackcloth and ashes and claim the promise of Isaiah 61:10! If you have ever needed someone to proclaim the good tidings of salvation to you, then turn off your religious broadcasting and get off of Face Book and Twitter which only multiply and magnify your discouragement and disappointment with the state of the world and the state of your life. Instead, you need to get "tuned" in to what the Lord has to say and what the Lord has to offer.

Have you heard the story about the Man who gave sight to the blind, healed the sick, fed the hungry, lifted up the paralyzed and straightened the bent and twisted? If your heart is broken He can mend it — but you must bring it to Him. In the midst of your suffering, know this, the Holy Ghost is the Comforter, the Lord Jesus Christ is the Savior and Redeemer, and God is a loving Father who seeks to restore you back to a right relationship with Him. Don the robe of righteousness and your garments of praise and begin to rejoice and sing praises to our mighty God.

One of our favorite songs to open worship on the Lord's Day is *What a Mighty God We Serve* by Clara M. Brooks and Barney E. Warren*:*

Our Father's wondrous works we see
In the earth and sea and sky;
He rules o'er all in majesty,
From His royal throne on high.

> What a mighty God we serve!
> What a mighty God we serve!
> Reigning now above on his throne of love,
> What a mighty God we serve!

The raging winds and waves are calm,
When He says to them, "Be still";
The heavens praise Him in a psalm,
And the angels do His will.

> He maketh worlds by His command,
> Weighs the mountains great and high;
> Creates the waters in His hand,
> Spans the lofty starlit sky.

Our God, to save from sin's control,
Gave His Son a sacrifice;
His grace, abounding in the soul,
Makes the earth a paradise.

-Worship the Lord: Hymnal of the Church of God, Warner Press, 46.

Prayer

What a mighty God we serve! We are weak but you are strong. We thank you for your everlasting love. You have called us to be holy. You have provided an Advocate for us if we fall short. You came to heal our broken hearts and set us free. Thank you for such love. Help us this week to extend that love to others. Help us to remember the words of the radio preacher as he closed each broadcast, "Be nice to everyone because everyone is having a tough time." Amen.

Parting Thought
We Praise What We Enjoy.
We delight to praise because the praise not merely expresses but completes the enjoyment.
In such manner, we praise our God!

For further study in the Book of Isaiah ...

ISAIAH, PRINCE OF PROPHETS
by Dr. Kenneth E. Jones

ISBN 9781604161830 Softcover $15
ISBN 9781604161847 Hardcover $25
S&H $5

REFORMATION PUBLISHERS

14 S. Queen Street • Mt. Sterling, KY 40353
1-800-765-2464 • rpublisher@aol.com
www.reformationpublishers.com

OCTOBER 2, 2016 · WEEK 5

THE DIVINE IMPRINT OF GOD

Bible Passage: Hebrews 1:1 - 9

Key Verse - Hebrews 1:3
Who being the brightness of his glory, and the express image of his person, and upholding all things by the word of his power, when he had by himself
purged our sins, sat down on the right hand of the Majesty on high;
KJV

Introduction and Background

Hebrews, along with 1st John, are the only letters in the New Testament which do not start with a greeting. Written in sermon style or as an essay, Hebrews has many references to the Old Testament. Hebrews is regarded by many commentators to be anonymous. There are a number of characteristic Pauline marks within its content indicating Paul may be its author. It has also been attributed to Barnabas, Apollo, and even to Luke. With regard to location and date it would appear that it was written before A.D. 95 for it has been quoted by Clement I, also known as St. Clement of Rome, who held office as Bishop of Rome from A.D. 88 to his death in A.D. 99. Clement is considered to be the first of the Apostolic Fathers. There is no reference to the Roman invasion of Palestine (A.D. 66-70) or the siege of the city by Titus found in the book. In fact, it seems to suggest that temple worship continued at the time of its writing. That would mean that most likely the letter was written around A.D. 64 – 65. The purpose of the letter was to specifically explain why the new Jewish believers in the audience should continue to hold on to their faith in Christ because of the superiority of Christ in every way to that of the Law.

A prophet is someone who speaks on God's behalf and communicates His message to the people. Prophets have no authority or power of their own; their authority is attained solely through the Holy Spirit. To be a prophet meant that he or she could not be intimately involved with their designated audience. While Moses' work as a prophet, preacher, and priest is unquestioned and applauded, the writer boldly proclaims that the One whom they now worship, Jesus Christ, a greater than Solomon or Jonah is here *(Matthew 12:41- 42; Luke 11:31 - 32)*. A greater prophet than Moses has come on the scene and His name is Jesus Christ, a fulfilment of prophecy **(Hebrews 3)**. He has power and authority of His own. This Unit of lessons will deal with **"The Sovereignty of Jesus."**

The Eminence of Jesus
Hebrews 1:1-4

1 God, who at sundry times and in divers manners spake in time past unto the fathers by the prophets,
2 Hath in these last days spoken unto us by his Son, whom he hath appointed heir of all things, by whom also he made the worlds;
3 Who being the brightness of his glory, and the express image of his person, and upholding all things by the word of his power, when he had by himself purged our sins, sat down on the right hand of the Majesty on high;
4 Being made so much better than the angels, as he hath by inheritance obtained a more excellent name than they. KJV

The writer of Hebrews divides the time between before Christ and after Christ using the terminology "in time past" and "in these last days." These verses relate to God's previous revelation in the Old Testament through the prophets and His presence through Jesus Christ in the New Testament. In the Old Testament, God used prophets to deliver His message to the targeted people and parties under the old covenant. With the coming of Jesus, He establishes a new communication and a new covenant. The term "last days" describes a messianic era. By definition the word *eminence* (**EM** eh nence) means:

1. A position of great distinction or superiority.
2. A rise of high ground, a hill.

3. A person of high station or great achievements.
4. A projecting protuberance from the surface of a body part.

For today, meaning number one will be the meaning for our consideration in this lesson. To the Jewish mind when the "last" or "final" days were spoken of, they believed the Messiah's presence would be the beginning of God's new earthly kingdom. It would bring freedom from political oppression by the Romans and world peace. Instead, Jesus founded a godly, spiritual kingdom and brought peace for the soul of man, all the while demonstrating His godly uniqueness. The writer places before us seven facts to show Jesus' superior greatness. (1) He is deemed the "heir" of creation. (2) He is the creator of all things made. (3) His transcendence reveals God's glory. This idea of God transcendent runs through the whole Bible. Daniel's encounter with God was probably the most dreadful and wonderful of them all. The prophet Daniel lifted up his eyes and saw One whose **"body also was like the beryl, and his face as the appearance of lightning, and his eyes as lamps of fire, and his arms and his feet like in colour to polished brass, and the voice of his words like the voice of a multitude"** *(Daniel 10:6).* (4) He is the exact imprint of God. (5) He is the personified Word of God. (6) He is the high priest who provided sacrifice for our sins. (7) He is seated on the eternal throne at God's **(His Father)** right hand.

Ponder Points

What stories of God and His work in Old Testament times speak especially and are meaningful to you? There are stories of deliverance, judgment, revelation and transformation. Share with the class your favorite stories.

The Angels Acknowledge the Superiority of the Son
Hebrews 1:5-9

5 For unto which of the angels said he at any time, Thou art my Son, this day have I begotten thee? And again, I will be to him a Father, and he shall be to me a Son?

6 And again, when he bringeth in the firstbegotten into the world, he saith, And let all the angels of God worship him.

7 And of the angels he saith, Who maketh his angels spirits, and his ministers a flame of fire.

8 But unto the Son he saith, Thy throne, O God, is for ever and ever: a sceptre of righteousness is the sceptre of thy kingdom.

9 Thou hast loved righteousness, and hated iniquity; therefore God, even thy God, hath anointed thee with the oil of gladness above thy fellows. *KJV*

Angels are members of the heavenly order of beings. As members of an order of heavenly beings, they are superior to man in power and intelligence.

Psalms 8:4-5

4 What is man, that thou art mindful of him? and the

son of man, that thou visitest him?

5 For thou hast made him a little lower than the angels, and hast crowned him with glory and honour. *KJV*

Angels were created by God and by nature are spiritual beings *(Hebrews 1:14)*. Their nature is superior to human nature *(Hebrews 2:7)*, and they have superhuman power and knowledge *(2 Samuel 14:17, 20; 2 Peter 2:11)*. They are not, however, all-powerful and all-knowing *(Psalms 103:20; 2 Thessalonians 1:7)*.

Of special importance in the Old Testament is the **ANGEL OF THE LORD** *(Genesis 16:7; 22:11; 31:11)*. This angel is depicted as a visible manifestation of God Himself. He has powers and characteristics that belong only to God, such as the power to forgive sins *(Exodus 23:20-21)*. His similarities to Jesus lead most scholars to conclude that He is a Christophany or Theophany, which is a physical manifestation of the living Word present with God at the creation of the world *(John 1:1,14)*.

When visible to human beings, angels consistently appear in human form *(Genesis 18:2; Daniel 10:18; Zechariah 2:1)*. Sometimes, however, their appearance inspire awe *(Judges 13:6; Matthew 28:3-4; Luke 24:4)*. Angels are never known to appear to wicked people – only to those whom the Bible view as good, such as Abraham, Moses, David, Daniel, Jesus, Peter, and Paul. They are charged with caring for such people and serving them in times of need *(Psalms 91:11-12; Hebrews 1:14)*.

They also guide and instruct good people *(Genesis 24:7, 40; Exodus 14:19)*. Angels also protect the people of God *(Exodus 14:19-20; Daniel 3:28; Matthew 26:53)*. They meet a wide variety of human needs, sometimes they deliver the people of God from danger *(Acts 5:19; 12:6-11)*.

Although they are not the objects of salvation, angels are interested in the salvation of human beings *(Luke 15:10; 1 Corinthians 4:9)*. They also were particularly active in the events surrounding the birth and resurrection of Jesus *(Matthew 1:20; 2:13, 19; 28:2; Luke 1:11-38; 2:9-15; 22:43; 24:23; John 20:12)*. The frequency with which angels participate in human affairs has diminished since Pentecost, probably because of the larger role played by the Holy Spirit in the lives of Christians since then. Angels are quite real, and they play a vital part in God's plan for the world.

The writer of Hebrews asks a couple of questions based on citations from the Old Testament. The first: **"For unto which of the angels said he at any time, Thou art my Son, this day have I begotten thee"** *(Hebrews 1:5 – KJV)*? Here the writer is preparing his readers to better understand the Sonship of Jesus Christ to the heavenly Father. No one but Christ can claim this type of inheritance. But the writer goes further, the Messiah's position as Son will be acknowledged by those whose job it is to give honor and glory to their Creator. In this instance, they will worship the Father's Son for He is the

Maker of all things that were made. The focus now is on God's Son, who is sitting at His right hand. The author continues explaining Jesus' eminence through His divinity. To totally reinforce Jesus's divinity, the writer utilizes several quotes from the Old Testament, one of them being Psalm 45:6 -7: "Thy throne, O God, is for ever and ever: the sceptre of thy kingdom is a right sceptre" *KJV.* Indeed, Jesus is on the throne where He rules in righteousness.

Ponder Points

While certainly not exhaustive due to time and space constraints, in our brief comments about angel beings and their function, what mistaken beliefs about angels have you heard? Did anything that was shared help you to better understand angelic power and authority?

Conclusion

In our lesson today, Hebrew's author indicates that though God saw fit to appoint and send a list of individuals to deal with humanity's issues, Jesus was special when He arrived on the scene. He entered this world by a supernatural birth for He was a supernatural being. Others before Jesus had an ordinary sense about them. Jesus was the embodiment of God and possessed God's power *(Hebrews 1:3)*. Distinguishing Jesus above all others was His identity as "heir" of God the Father. That is special, it belongs to no other! That means that when Jesus shows up in our lives — unlike others when they have shown up — it is a special encounter. Nobody can do what Jesus does to get us out of where we have gotten ourselves. He is the One and Only Son of God and as such our One and Only Savior and Redeemer.

F.G. Smith said, "If you have something that you can run without God's help, then you have the wrong thing."

Prayer

Lord, thank you for coming to earth for our salvation. We recognize you as our only Savior. As the little child said, "You were the best picture God ever took." Amen.

Parting Thought

One hour with God infinitely exceeds all the delight and pleasures of this lower world.

OCTOBER 9, 2016 · WEEK 6

BUILDER OF THE HOUSE

Bible Passage: Hebrews 3:1-6; Matthew 7:24 - 29

Key Verse - Hebrews 3:3

For this man was counted worthy of more glory than Moses, inasmuch as he who hath builded the house hath more honour than the house.
KJV

Introduction and Background

Part of our text this week is found in Hebrews and the background for the Hebrew portion was covered in last week's Lesson Background. The rest of our text for this week comes from Matthew and is at the end of that famous Sermon on the Mount. This lowly son of a carpenter from the obscure village of Nazareth was in the first year of His three years of earthly ministry. He was teaching what it means to be subjects of God's kingdom. He spoke with authority that could only come from God. To listen to Jesus and obey meant blessing; to ignore Him and write Him off meant ruin.

Hebrews presented Jesus as the divine Son of God,

"heir to the Father". Matthew shows Jesus as One-of-a-Kind. His greatness was revealed in all that He did and said. Together, both books declare that to follow Jesus and His teaching is to be in the presence of greatness.

Last week we compared Jesus, the divine Son of God, with angels. This week our Scriptures reveal the humanity of the Son of God and His mission. The commonality of these to passages of Scripture, Hebrews 3 and Matthew 7, is that both of them set forth the image of a house and its builder. The author of Hebrews points out "For every house is builded by some man; but he that built all things is God" *(Hebrews 3:4 – KJV)*. Matthew 7:24 states: "Therefore whosoever heareth these sayings of mine, and doeth them, I will liken him unto a wise man, which built his house upon a rock:"

Both Jesus and Moses were faithful builders — both built on rock! However today's lesson will show that "…. Moses verily was faithful in all his house, as a servant, … But Christ as a son over his own house; whose house are we,…." *(Hebrews 3:5 - 6 – KJV)*.

The Greatness of Jesus
Hebrews 3:1-6

1. Wherefore, holy brethren, partakers of the heavenly calling, consider the Apostle and High Priest of our profession, Christ Jesus;
2. Who was faithful to him that appointed him, as also Moses was faithful in all his house.

3   For this man was counted worthy of more glory than Moses, inasmuch as he who hath builded the house hath more honour than the house.
4   For every house is builded by some man; but he that built all things is God.
5   And Moses verily was faithful in all his house, as a servant, for a testimony of those things which were to be spoken after;
6   But Christ as a son over his own house; whose house are we, if we hold fast the confidence and the rejoicing of the hope firm unto the end. *KJV*

The writer of Hebrews launches his words to his listeners as a family of believers. He is reminding his hearers to remember who they are in Christ Jesus. When Jesus died on Calvary and rose from the dead on that third day morning, all who believed Him to be who He said He was were made holy, sanctified by His shed blood. They are now the sons and daughters of God born into His family. In doing this the Hebrew writer is guiding the minds of his hearers and readers to think of themselves from a spiritual perspective and not from an earthly one.

Notice if you will the two titles which he applies to Jesus: Apostle and High Priest (v.1). An apostle – *apostolos* (ap-os'-tol-os) – is a messenger. This is a title befitting of Jesus because He was sent from God to a dark and dying world to reconcile fallen man back to God and to defeat death by bring life. The second title given to Jesus is "high priest" – *archiereus* (ar-khee-er-yuce') – The High Priest was the religious leader of the people of Israel. He had to be holy at all times because he was the mediator between God and his people. Dr. Lillie S. McCutcheon preached, "A priest lifts man up to God and brings God down to man." He was also responsible for overseeing the priests who served in the temple under his direction.

Then, the writer follows with a direct comparison between Christ and Moses. They were both faithful in the discharge of their duties, yet Jesus was counted worthy of more glory than Moses. Why was this? The writer uses the analogy of a builder and the raising of a house. The house may be beautiful and the design wonderful, but sooner than later someone is going to ask, "Who built the house?" This is because the builder of the house has more honor than the house itself! The comparison is not to belittle Moses, it is to point out that Moses could not do what Christ as the Son of God could do. Although Moses was faithful to the household of God, his faithfulness was to show devotion to God. Jesus' faithfulness is more esteemed because He is the Son, the "heir of the owner of the house". As such He is "over" the house and the household. The household is the personification of the body of believers both in the Old Testament and the New Testament which is the church.

Ponder Points

It goes without saying that Moses had a calling from God to shepherd His people on their wilderness journey. It is an understatement that Jesus was on mission from heaven to earth. What are some ways for you to be faithful servants such as Moses and Jesus and to live out your calling as children of the Lord? Would being an example of the believer be one way? How about witnessing and leading people to Christ in personal evangelism?

The Teachings of Jesus
Matthew 7:24-27

24 Therefore whosoever heareth these sayings of mine, and doeth them, I will liken him unto a wise man, which built his house upon a rock:
25 And the rain descended, and the floods came, and the winds blew, and beat upon that house; and it fell not: for it was founded upon a rock.
26 And every one that heareth these sayings of mine, and doeth them not, shall be likened unto a foolish man, which built his house upon the sand:
27 And the rain descended, and the floods came, and the winds blew, and beat upon that house; and it fell: and great was the fall of it. *KJV*

These verses contain serious spiritual warnings and instructions. Jesus says to those crowded around Him that when you build a house you should build on a solid foundation such as "rock". The reason that you build on rock is that it is strong, it is stable and it can hold the weight of the building. That means that heavy rainstorms and unpredictable high winds will not cause the structure to shift on its foundation and fall. One such skyscraper, the Millennium Tower, the most expensive real estate in all of San Francisco, is leaning 16 inches because of a poor foundation. When you hear the Word of Jesus, the Teacher, and begin to practice His teachings, you are building your spiritual house on a spiritual and moral foundation. When the winds of controversy blow and begin to assault your house it will stand up to the wind. When the rainstorm of complacency blows into your mental and moral neighborhood it will not drown your confidence or sink you sanity or security. Heeding the lessons of the Sermon on the Mount will bring security; disobedience will bring defeat, destruction and eventual collapse.

This parable invites us to a life of obedience. Words are of no value unless they are acted upon. We should HEAR the Word and then DO the Word. It is in the doing that we are building. It is good to know that we can build our spiritual homes in and on Jesus. It is good to know that the lot or land has been paid for at Calvary by the shed blood of God's Lamb. Jesus paid it all!

Conclusion

Jesus said,

> John 14:6
> I am the way, the truth, and the life: no man cometh unto the Father, but by me. *KJV*

The verse is clear; it leaves no room for question. If you want to make heaven your home you are going to have to come God's way. There is no other, and there is no other name through which you can be saved. Buddha will not get the job done. Krishna, Allah, Mohammed all are ladders which are too short. **"Neither is there salvation in any other: for there is none other name under heaven given among men, whereby we must be saved "** *(Acts 4:12 KJV)*.

According to the writer of Hebrews even though Moses was faithful in carrying out his assignment given to him by God, he had moments when he was not in full obedience to the task at hand. Jesus, on the other hand, was faithful not only to the assignment given Him, but He was also a faithful Ruler over God's house. The writer encourages his readers to stay firm in their faith. He tells them not to waver because when one steps away from the truth, he becomes susceptible to strong delusions from the enemy. Every believer should not only know the Word of God, but also do their very best to live out its precepts. When we do, we will not be called foolish, but rather we will reflect the wisdom of God in our living.

The Church of God has many favorite Bible passages. One is found in Matt. 16:18 where Jesus said, "...I will build my church and gates of hell shall not prevail against it." He is the Builder of the house, the church of God. A carpenter shop in Nazareth was just a foretaste, an apprenticeship, of what was to come as the Builder of the New Testament Church.

Prayer

While it may be difficult to find good builders, contractors today to start and finish the job, thank you Lord that you started building the church of God a long time ago. You have been faithful to keep building her down through the centuries. Now, you want the New Testament to go forward. We feel so out of place and out of touch at times. We dislike so many changes. We feel inadequate. But, You have a house to finish building. So, may we trust You to help us reach our generation, which has so many problems, with the gospel. Amen.

Parting Thought

The cost of obedience is nothing
compared to the cost of disobedience.

OCTOBER 16, 2016 · WEEK 7

OUR GREAT HIGH PRIEST

Bible Passage: Hebrews 4:14-16, Hebrews 5:1-10

Key Verse -Hebrews 4:14
Seeing then that we have a great high priest, that is passed into the heavens, Jesus the Son of God, let us hold fast our profession.

Introduction and Background

At first every man was his own priest, and presented his own sacrifices before God. Afterwards that office devolved on the head of the family, as in the cases of Noah *(Genesis 8:20)*, Abraham *(Genesis12:7; 13:4)*, Isaac *(26:25)*, Jacob *(31:54)*, and Job *(Job 1:5)*.

The name High Priest occurs as applied to Melchizedec *(Genesis 14:18)*. Under the Levitical arrangements the office of the priesthood was limited to the tribe of Levi, and then to only one family of that tribe, the family of Aaron. Certain laws respecting the qualifications of priests are given in Leviticus 21:16-23. There are ordinances also regarding the priests' dress *(Exodus 28:40-43)* and the manner of their consecration to the office *(Genesis 29:1-*

37). Israel's High Priest was one of many priests who offered sacrifices of various kinds on the sacred altar. But ONCE a year, on the Day of Atonement, only the High Priest officiated at the special sacrifice. Atonement meant a covering for sin and sacrifices were made on that day to cover the sins of the people for another year.

On that occasion the High Priest first offered the sacrifice of a bullock for himself and for his house. The animal's life was offered as a substitute, taking the punishment in place of the High Priest and his household for their sins *(Leviticus 16:6)*. The High Priest also cast lots to determine which of the two goats would be sacrificed and which would be sent away into the wilderness bearing the sin debt of the nation as the scapegoat *(Leviticus 16:7-10)*. The High Priest sprinkled blood of the sacrificed bullock and goat on the "mercy seat" which was behind the veil in the "Holy of Holies" or "the most holy place," *(Exodus 26:34)*. Only on this one day of the year did anyone enter that room.

The essence of the Day of Atonement therefore was that of a sacrifice of substitution, the lives of innocent animals were given in place of the lives of human sinners. God ordained the High Priest to this ministry and only one who occupied this office that God created could preside over this sacred rite. The whole priestly system of the Jews was typical. It was a shadow of the body of sacrifice of Christ. The priests all prefigured the great High Priest who offered "one sacrifice for sins" "once for all" *(Hebrews*

10:10, 12). There is now no human priesthood. The term "priest" is applied to believers *(1 Peter 2:9; Revelation 1:6)*. All true believers are now "kings and priests unto God." As priests, we have free access into the holiest of all through our eternal High Priest Jesus Christ, where we can offer up the sacrifices of praise and thanksgiving, and the sacrifices of grateful service from day to day.

As we turn to our lesson for today, we will see that Jesus was a superior High Priest because of His empathy for our human dilemma. He was not like the high priests who were chosen and born of the flesh, This High Priest came from heaven. He ascended again to heaven, but He hasn't forgotten the task given to Him by His Father. In heaven, at God's right hand, He makes intercession for us before the throne.

Jesus, Our Great High Priest
Hebrews 4:14-16

14 Seeing then that we have a great high priest, that is passed into the heavens, Jesus the Son of God, let us hold fast our profession.

15 Fr we have not an high priest which cannot be touched with the feeling of our infirmities; but was in all points tempted like as we are, yet without sin.

16 Let us therefore come boldly unto the throne of grace, that we may obtain mercy, and find grace to help in time of need. *KJV*

Having already argued the superiority of Jesus, the

writer says that "we have a great high priest who has passed into the heavens" *(v. 14)*. Moses was the leader of the Mosaic system and he possessed supreme religious authority. But the writer makes Jesus greater than Moses, indeed greater than Aaron, or any human high priest. What is meant by "passed into the heavens"? Indeed the Aaronic high priest passed behind the veil into the "Holy of Holies" before the Ark of the Covenant one day a year, but Jesus, of the Melchisedecian (mel **KEZ** uh dek ee un) priesthood has passed through the veil of death and into the very presence of God on His throne to make an eternal atonement that stands for ALL time *(Hebrews 7:27)* at the "mercy seat" standing before God's throne.

Because of what Jesus accomplished through His death, burial, and resurrection, He is seated at the right hand of the Father which indicates that the work or redemption is forever finished and our High Priest does not have to rise to His feet to make another sacrifice, "It Is Finished!" This makes Jesus more than qualified to represent God to the people and the people to God. We have a Savior Who was at all points tempted or tried as we are but He did not sin. As we stand in His righteousness, we can come boldly to the throne of grace and receive what we need from God in the name of our Redeemer.

Ponder Points

How does the fact that Jesus has undergone temptation and trial, more severe that any human — yet remained sinless — impact you personally? By His example has it helped you to become an example? By His prayer, submission and yielding, has this spoken to you about your own submission to the Father's will? How can we better communicate that Christ shares and understands our weaknesses?

Jesus and Earthly High Priests
Hebrews 5:1-5

1 For every high priest taken from among men is ordained for men in things pertaining to God, that he may offer both gifts and sacrifices for sins:
2 Who can have compassion on the ignorant, and on them that are out of the way; for that he himself also is compassed with infirmity.
3 And by reason hereof he ought, as for the people, so also for himself, to offer for sins.
4 And no man taketh this honour unto himself, but he that is called of God, as was Aaron.
5 So also Christ glorified not himself to be made an high priest; but he that said unto him, Thou art my Son, to day have I begotten thee. *KJV*

The earthly high priest was human. Because of this, strict instructions were put in place for him and the ones for whom he was interceding. This was a serious office and not taken lightly. This responsibility was not self-assumed, God was the one that made the call and as such the high priest was not free to do whatever he chose with respect to the people and more importantly before God. Under Mosaic Law, God set apart the high priest to represent Himself to the people and the people to Him. God established the priesthood to come from the lineage of Aaron, Moses' older brother. He wore special clothing that was designed for the office and each piece had a significant meaning in behalf of his ministry before the people. All of this was a foreshadowing of the eternal High Priest who was to come from the Father, who was Jesus Christ. Once a year when the earthly high priest stepped behind the veil into the "Holy of Holies" he laid aside all of the high priest regalia and clothing and stepped into the presence of the Shekinah glory of God before the mercy seat as a mere man to offer sin for himself and his house. Our eternal High Priest laid aside His eternal garments of the Order of Melchisedec and stepped down through time to minister, suffer, bear our burdens and represent us before the Father and then to die our death for us. On that third and glorious day, He arose victorious over death, hell and the grave. For 40 days He preached the message of the present kingdom and then from that Mount of Ascension He returned to heaven to pick up His eternal robes as the High Priest of the Melchisedecian priesthood to become our priest forever representing us before our holy God.

Jesus and Melchisedec High Priest Forever
Hebrews 5:6-8

6   As he saith also in another place, Thou art a priest

for ever after the order of Melchisedec.
7   Who in the days of his flesh, when he had offered up prayers and supplications with strong crying and tears unto him that was able to save him from death, and was heard in that he feared;
8   Though he were a Son, yet learned he obedience by the things which he suffered;   *KJV*

While the Aaronic priesthood was God-ordained and sufficient for the time, it was by no means perfect because it was functioned and filled by men who knew sin, and therefore, were subjected to death. This meant a priesthood that was ever changing, with all that resulted from those changes. God knew this and had planned a more perfect priesthood which could only come into being in the fullness of His time, for God works on His divine schedule, not the frameworks of men.

We also notice this man, Melchizedec, who was king of Salem and priest of the most high God, was both a king and a priest, which could not apply to the Jewish economy. He was king of a city on the earth, but he was priest of God, who is in heaven! The man was greater than Abraham — because Abraham paid tithes to him, and he also had authority from God to put a blessing on Abraham. Paul tells us the less is blessed by the greater!

Melchisedec is a foreshadowing of Christ because he combined kingship and priesthood in his person; Jesus remains in the office of Priest and King forever, which is why we call Him Lord. Jesus was faithful in the days of His humanity by staying in a posture of prayerful submission and obedience to God. Although He is the Son of God, He still suffered all the experiences of man and knows what is in man and what it takes to obey God. Later, the author of Hebrews writes that Christ entered into the heavenly "Holy of Holies" to apply His blood on the mercy seat on our behalf and now remains in the presence of God to make intercession for us *(Hebrews 9:11 - 12)*.

After many years of rolling this passage around in my mind and in my heart, in reading, studying, and listening to what myriads of commentators have said and hold about Melchizedec, I do not see any way to get around taking the words of Paul in Hebrews at face value. He says that Melchizedec was without father and without mother – without decent or pedigree from any race or tribe known among men, and without beginning or infancy of day, and that he never died, but lived on without dying. Commentators have tried to sidestep these words in all sorts of ways by making them refer only to the character of his priesthood. But I do not see how it is possible to avoid taking these words just as they read.

Hebrew 7:3

> 3 Without father, without mother, without descent, having neither beginning of days, nor end of life; but made like unto the Son of God; abideth a priest continually. KJV

Jesus, in speaking of John the Baptist, says that of men that are born of women there had never been a greater then John the Baptist. In using these words, Jesus intimates that there are men, or have been men, that were not born of women. We know that Adam was not born of woman, and when the apostle tells us that Melchizedec had no father and no mother, I believe the words mean exactly what they say, and that Melchizedec was a man come from God in the time in which Abraham lived.

Now consider the characteristics of this new "**order**" of the priesthood. There were many High Priests and priests who officiated under the Aaronic Priesthood, all of them were subject to death, but **ONLY ONE, Melchisedec**! He stood out — and stands out like the moon against the stars of the night in the Old Testament. But when the morning ***"SUN"*** of the New Testament had risen, the **ONE GREAT ETERNAL HIGH PRIEST** — Jesus — rose like the sun, subduing all other lights. All the others had only borne a dim reflection of Him!

Mal 4:2

But unto you that fear my name shall the Sun of righteousness arise with healing in his wings;" *KJV*.

Conclusion

The greatest feeling in the world is the feeling that we are fulfilling the God ordained purpose for our lives. It doesn't matter the time required or the task being carried out, doing God's will brings great joy and satisfaction to the soul. When we have done the best that we can, with all that we have, for as long as we could, and with all of our might, God is pleased with our efforts.

The next best feeling is to know that we have a High Priest and an Advocate before the Father that can intercede for us and who knows what is in us and what we are going through. He understands personally. He invites us to trust Him, and when we do, our "Why?" questions can be turned into "What do you want me to learn?" questions. If you ever need a lawyer, it is always good to have one who is able to best represent your interests. Jesus is the One!

Prayer

We thank you Lord for taking our place on Calvary. You paid the ultimate price for our salvation. You suffered for us that we might have eternal life. Please forgive our complaining when we are asked to suffer a little for your cause. Amen.

Parting Thought

The question, *"What is meant by intercession?"* being asked in a Sunday school class, one of the children replied, *"Speaking a word to God for us, sir."*

OCTOBER 23, 2016 · WEEK 8

THE HIGH PRIEST FOREVER

Bible Passage: Hebrews 7:1- 3, 18 - 28

Key Verse - Hebrews 7:24
But this man, because he continueth ever, hath an unchangeable priesthood.

Introduction and Background

Last week the writer of this letter of Hebrews referred to Jesus:

Hebrews 7:17
Thou art a priest for ever after the order of Melchisedec.
KJV

quoting Psalm 110:4. He did not however elaborate on that point at great length. That will take place with today's lesson on "The High Priest Forever." Melchisedec appears in the Old Testament only in Genesis 14 and Psalm 110, with his name spelled *Melchizedek* (mel **KIZ** eh deck) in both places. These passages inform us of his great status, but other than that little information is given about who he is. Psalm 110 is looking forward to the Messiah and the deliverance He will bring about when He is comes. Psalm 110:4 affirms that "The Lord hath sworn, and will not repent, Thou art a priest for ever after the order of Melchizedek" *(KJV)*. He held the offices of both king and priest. He is portrayed as greater than Levitical priests of the order of Aaron. He blessed Abraham on his return from rescuing Lot and his family from the kings of Sodom. We know nothing of his ancestry, priestly pedigree, birth or death, thereby echoing the eternal existence and unending priesthood of Christ. His name spelled Melchizedek, means "King of Righteousness." Salem, the name of his city, signified "peace." This is the ancient name of the Jebusite city-state deriving from the Hebrew word "*shalom*" (**SHALL** loam) meaning peace, blessing and well-being. This city taken by King David became the city of the king and was renamed Jerusalem. Thus as king of peace, he typified Christ, the Prince of Peace, the One whose saving work reconciles God and humankind. It is clear that Melchizekek's priesthood was a model for how the church understands the priesthood of Christ. So it is important for us to consider what the writer of Hebrews has to say with great care.

An Unending Life
Hebrews 7:1-3

1 For this Melchisedec, king of Salem, priest of the most high God, who met Abraham returning from the slaughter of the kings, and blessed him;
2 To whom also Abraham gave a tenth part of all;

first being by interpretation King of righteousness, and after that also King of Salem, which is, King of peace;
3 Without father, without mother, without descent, having neither beginning of days, nor end of life; but made like unto the Son of God; abideth a priest continually. *KJV*

Today's text, drawn from chapter seven, elaborates on "This king Melchizedek of Salem...". While this sounds odd to us, remember those first readers and Hebrew hearers would have been familiar with this story. By connecting Melchizedek to "the Most High God," the writer shows Melchizedek had God's approval and sanction as one of His called priests.

The Levitical priests were respected by the people as godly leaders and teachers of the Law of Moses. In addition to having a godly legacy and reputation, the priests served a crucial role for the people in the Tabernacle and the Temple. They were intermediaries between the people and God, offering sacrifices. Hebrews 7 places before the Hebrew readers and hearers the reality that Jesus was a superior High Priest in the line of Melchizedek. To make the case, Hebrews 7 argues that Jesus' priestly credential or degree was issued from a superior school. That is, Jesus was from the "**spiritual Ivy League**" of Melchizedek and not from the "**diploma mill**" of the Levites and the Aaronic school of priests. The author seemingly plays down the Aaronic priesthood and lifts up the Melchisedecian school of which Jesus was High Priest of that ancient order. Long before the Law and long before Aaron and the Levitical priesthood there was Melchisedec, a "priest of the Most High God" *(Hebrews 7:1).*

An Unbreakable Oath
Hebrews 7:19-22

19 For the law made nothing perfect, but the bringing in of a better hope did; by the which we draw nigh unto God.
20 And inasmuch as not without an oath he was made priest:
21 (For those priests were made without an oath; but this with an oath by him that said unto him, The Lord sware and will not repent, Thou art a priest for ever after the order of Melchisedec:)
22 By so much was Jesus made a surety of a better testament.

Jesus being "made an high priest for ever after the order of Melchisedec" *(Hebrews 6:20 – KJV).* This new priesthood, marked by many changes, had two results: it abolished the old priesthood, and it introduced a new and better hope. So, was the writer pointing out that the Law was not intended to save anyone, but only to point out their failings and sin? He makes it crystal clear in verse 19 – "For the law made nothing perfect." As a matter of fact, it pointed out just how imperfect everyone was, even the priests of Aaron's school.

We have an unchanging priest — "Jesus Christ, the same yesterday, and to-day, and for ever" (Heb. 13:9). He is kind, gentle, and One Who is touched with the feelings of our infirmities. He is consecrated by an oath which cannot be altered! This ought to bring joy to our hearts and a *"Hallelujah! Glory!"* to our lips for such a wonderful Savior! The Melchisedecian priesthood was instituted with an oath *(20 - 21)*. Verse twenty-one tells us that the Aaronic/Levitical priests were made priests without an oath, but the Melchisedecian order was made **"with an oath."** This oath is nothing more or less than the entire and irreversible consecration to the eternal will of God which no one but a child of God can make. When we do this there is a double avouchment that takes place.

Deut 26:17-18

17 Thou hast avouched the Lord this day to be thy God, and to walk in his ways, and to keep his statutes, and his commandments, and his judgments, and to hearken unto his voice:
18 And the Lord hath avouched thee this day to be his peculiar People,

We promise ourselves and we promise God to be His, and His alone, for the rest of our days and He promises us that He will be our everlasting Father. A man can be born and grow up to be a citizen without ever taking any oath of allegiance, but when he joins the armed forces, and unites the office of a soldier to that of a citizen it must be done with an oath! The very idea of being a soldier implies laying one's life on the line and requires a degree of loyalty greater than mere citizenship. Conversion or the "**New Birth**" makes us citizens of God's kingdom, and the "**sanctifying**" in-filling of the Holy Spirit constitutes us soldiers. This happens when we release our control and we turn over full control of our bodies to the Lord and present ourselves as a gift for Him to use, mold, and make into what He wants us to be. With this work of sanctification we enter this higher rank of loyalty with an oath of eternal fidelity. This is the order of Melchisedec.

An Unchangeable Priesthood
Hebrews 7:23-28

23 And they truly were many priests, because they were not suffered to continue by reason of death:

24 But this man, because he continueth ever, hath an

unchangeable priesthood.

25 Wherefore he is able also to save them to the uttermost that come unto God by him, seeing he ever liveth to make intercession for them.

26 For such an high priest became us, who is holy, harmless, undefiled, separate from sinners, and made higher than the heavens;

27 Who needeth not daily, as those high priests, to offer up sacrifice, first for his own sins, and then for the people's: for this he did once, when he offered up himself.

28 For the law maketh men high priests which have infirmity; but the word of the oath, which was since the law, maketh the Son, who is consecrated for evermore. *KJV*

Now that the writer has shown the superiority of Melchizedek's priesthood over the Levitical-Aaronic priesthood, as well as the imperfections of this earthly order of priests, he moves to another area in which Jesus is superior. In order that the office of high priest be adequately filled on a continual basis, many priests were needed because their life spans were limited. But this man, Jesus, holds His priesthood permanently because He continues to live forever *(v. 24)*. According to verse 25, this Mediator of the new covenant **"ever liveth to make intercession for them."** Christ's priesthood was permanent and unchangeable, where the priests of the Law died, leaving a vacancy in the priesthood until they were replaced. At all times, in all things Jesus is available to aide us and to intercede for us.

Finally, verses 26 - 28 of our text speaks to us of the holiness of our High Priest who is holy, blameless, undefiled, and separated from sinners. The high priests of the Levitical system had to make constant sacrifices and consecrate themselves on a constant daily, hourly basis. Priests of the Law were mortal and sinful, so they had their share of physical infirmities and defects with which there was constant struggle. No lawful priest could have qualified to make atonement for sin and intercession for sinners, except Jesus Christ, who was altogether holy and ever at the ready.

Conclusion

Times of affliction and the discouragement they bring may make God feel distant and far away from where we are. Job certainly felt that way in his time of suffering and trial. Job longed for someone to help and we hear his call for a divine daysman in Job 9:32- 33:

> 32 For he is not a man, as I am, that I should answer him, and we should come together in judgment.
> 33 Neither is there any daysman betwixt us, that might lay his hand upon us both. *KJV*

Job's plaintive cry was back before the arrival of our eternal High Priest, Jesus Christ. How wonderful it is to know that the "**divine daysman**" has come and that God is present in our world and that He has brought a plan from the beginning to redeem not just the people of Israel, but all races, all nations, all languages, all people of all time back to the Creator. No one could have known what God was doing when Abraham first gave tithes to Melchizadek. Only the love of a God who cares for us could have made it apparent even so many centuries later through the life, death, and resurrection of His Son.

Jesus' promise to one day return to gather His church, the bride to Himself is something we do not have to wonder or worry about because our High Priest is under an oath to fullfill His promise to us. God cannot and will not change, so we are covered by His oath as our High Priest forever.

Prayer

Lord, you are our High Priest. You are our Savior. You are our Mediator. You are our Advocate. We know that we have the best counsel possible. We know your love motivates you to rule in our favor. When you died for our sins, you ruled in our favor. We will not fear an eternal sentence to hell. Instead, we look forward to the place you are preparing for us. You spent six days on the Creation we know. You have been over 2000 years preparing our eternal home. What an upgrade! Amen.

Parting Thought

Jesus is the "Yes" to every promise of God.

Vocabulary

Avouchment: Noun for verbs affirm, guarantee, admit
Daysman: Umpire, mediator

OCTOBER 30, 2016 · WEEK 9
REFORMATION SUNDAY

PIONEER AND PERFECTER OF OUR FAITH

Bible Passage: Hebrews 12:1-13

Key Verse - Hebrews 12:1-2

Wherefore seeing we also are compassed about with so great a cloud of witnesses, let us lay aside every weight, and the sin which doth so easily beset us, and let us run with patience the race that is set before us,

Looking unto Jesus the author and finisher of our faith; who for the joy that was set before him endured the cross, despising the shame, and is set down at the right hand of the throne of God.

Introduction and Background

The last portion of the letter to the Hebrews begins with an exhortation to faithfulness and a plea to resist apostasy. The writer has just cited many examples of people who had demonstrated great faith (Hebrews 11 – the Roll Call of Faith). They had persevered with patience. Chapter eleven provides us a brief history of people who demonstrated great faith in God, beginning in Genesis with Abel, and continuing with those who were "**tortured, refusing to turn from God in order to be free**" *(Hebrews 11:35)*. These people are a cloud of witnesses, people who believed God and testified to His faithfulness and power. The Greek word used for witness is *martus* (**MAR'**-toos), which can be translated as "**spectator, witness, or testifier.**"

At this point, we should recall that there are at least three reasons why this letter was written:

- Encourage those new Jewish Christians to hold on and not give up until Jesus returns.
- Encourage them to keep growing in grace and in the knowledge of the truth.
- Remind them that Jesus Christ is superior to the Law and the prophets.

Our Christian walk is an experience that shares a common source and destination, yet each of us will find our individual path drastically different. Some folk seem to be "**born saved**", particularly if they have a long heritage of Christian upbringing. Others experience a radical conversion as a result of their experiences and make a distinct decision to take up their cross and follow Jesus, changing their life's course completely to the shock of some and to the relief of others. The apostle Paul when he was Saul comes to mind. While we will all differ, we all have an equal opportunity to learn of Jesus, accept Him and to live victoriously by grace through faith in His name. Hebrews 12 helps us find our own path and way to victory here and hereafter.

Be Faithful
Hebrews 12:1-4

1 Wherefore seeing we also are compassed about with so great a cloud of witnesses, let us lay aside every weight, and the sin which doth so easily beset us, and let us run with patience the race that is set before us,
2 Looking unto Jesus the author and finisher of our faith; who for the joy that was set before him endured the cross, despising the shame, and is set down at the right hand of the throne of God.
3 For consider him that endured such contradiction of sinners against himself, lest ye be wearied and faint in your minds.
4 Ye have not yet resisted unto blood, striving against sin. *KJV*

As I am writing this lesson the 2016 Summer Olympics has just opened in Rio de Janeiro, Brazil. The various sports venues will be all the news for the next little while. The setting the writer uses in our text today is couched in athletic events common to the Greco-Roman times, similar to the Rio Games. There are runners and witnesses in his account. These "**witnesses**" were example of those who trusted God and lived for Him to the end. Their steadfastness encouraged others to do the same. The "**runners**" typifying his audience are encouraged to strip off any weight of any kind that would hinder them in their running for the Lord. Instead of being weighted down and encumbered, believers should run with endurance the race stretched out before them. Those who have gone before us have had their share of struggles, yet even so they have gone on, and now they are in the grandstands urging us to keep on pressing on. They surround us like the crowd in an arena surrounds the contestants in a game.

As with those faithful men and women of Hebrews 11, Jesus, "**the pioneer and perfecter of our faith**" encourages us to press forward to the finish line to gain the prize. Jesus with full knowledge of what lay before Him pressed on to Calvary, endured the Cross and despised the ridicule and stayed the course. He had a greater purpose in mind, "**the joy that was set before Him**" caused Him to focus on that joy and endure the suffering and He is now sitting at the Father's right hand. Jesus not only started the race, but He stayed the race, and He crossed the finish line. He is our ultimate example — the One who demonstrates what true faith looks like.

Ponder Points

What are some hindrances which you have laid aside

to better run the race before you. Would habits be considered weights, bad attitudes, sharp cutting words and tongues? How about staying constant and pressing onward and upward?

Be Disciplined
Hebrews 12:5-11

5 And ye have forgotten the exhortation which speaketh unto you as unto children, My son, despise not thou the chastening of the Lord, nor faint when thou art rebuked of him:

6 For whom the Lord loveth he chasteneth, and scourgeth every son whom he receiveth.

7 If ye endure chastening, God dealeth with you as with sons; for what son is he whom the father chasteneth not?

8 But if ye be without chastisement, whereof all are partakers, then are ye bastards, and not sons.

9 Furthermore we have had fathers of our flesh which corrected us, and we gave them reverence: shall we not much rather be in subjection unto the Father of spirits, and live?

10 For they verily for a few days chastened us after their own pleasure; but he for our profit, that we might be partakers of his holiness.

11 Now no chastening for the present seemeth to be joyous, but grievous: nevertheless afterward it yieldeth the peaceable fruit of righteousness unto them which are exercised thereby. *KJV*

In this portion of our Scripture the writer moves from a focus on the suffering of Christ. His metaphor shifts from a race and running to a fighter and a boxing match. In the death of Jesus the blood of the innocent was shed for the guilty. We may have struggled but we have not yet resisted to the shedding of our own blood. Even if it did culminate in martyrdom it would not be equivalent to Jesus' shedding His blood. The main thrust of this passage is that of "disciplined" from the Greek word *paideia* (pahee **DI** '-ah) which means "education, training, or correction." The writer is simply making his readers aware that trials and hardship are tools in God's hands to correct us, to teach us and to temper us. While unpleasant when under the goad of discipline it is a sign of God's love for us that He would train us, and correct us and even rebuke us that we might be found wholly righteous (living as saints should live). The author looks at how our human parents discipline us for our good. Why shouldn't we accept being disciplined by our heavenly Father?

Ponder Points

Can we know or tell when a hardship is a result of divine discipline or merely the natural consequences of our own actions? What may happen if we do not ask this question? What form might such discipline take — health, relational, financial, emotional?

Be Strong
Hebrews 12:11-12

11 Now no chastening for the present seemeth to be joyous, but grievous: nevertheless afterward it yieldeth the peaceable fruit of righteousness unto them which are exercised thereby.
12 Wherefore lift up the hands which hang down, and the feeble knees; *KJV*

Because of the examples set forth by the "cloud of witnesses" and by Christ, the "pioneer and perfecter of our faith", and the realization that many trials are allowed to make believers more like God, readers are then encouraged to stand firm and be strengthened. The writer knew that those who would read this letter were tired; tired of all that came along with publicly acknowledging that Jesus Christ is Lord in that 1st Century Greco-Roman world. These are weary people with tired and sagging hands, tired and sagging hearts and weary knees. This author endeavors to encourage his readers to lift up sagging hands in praise and thanksgiving and in doing so sagging spirits may be given a jump start to get them back in a praising mode.

Anything worth having requires work, both to get it as well as to keep it and maintain it. Regardless of what slows us down, the goal is to progress toward the goal. Keep walking, keep pushing back those things that would impede our moving forward.

Let the words of this great song of the Church of God inspire you:

I'm Going On

I mean to go right on
Until the crown is won;
I mean to fight the fight of faith
Till life on earth is done.
I'll never more turn back,
Defeat I shall not know,
For God will give me victory,
If onward I shall go.

    I'm going on, I'm going on,
    Unto the final triumph, I'm going on.

Should opposition come,
Should foes obstruct my way,
Should persecution's fires be lit
As in the ancient day;
With Jesus by my side,
His peace within my soul,
No matter if the battle's hot,
I mean to win the goal.

I see a shining crown
Awaiting over there,
I see a mansion all prepared
And decked with beauties rare:
Shall that which intervenes
Deprive me of my right?
Nay, on I'll go until I reach
That city of delight.

Then forward let us go,
Our hearts with love aflame,
Our snowy banner borne aloft,
Inscribed with Jesus' name.
The hosts of evil flee,
And heaven's open gates
Invite me now to hasten where
Eternal glory waits.

-Naylor, Charles W. and Andrew L. Byers. Worship the Lord: Hymnal of the Church of God, Warner Press, 685.

Conclusion

Many talk about discipline or about being disciplined, but few people truly understand or appreciate the process. Discipline involves training, education, and correction, and it is accomplished in various ways. Sometime it is through hardship, trials, pain, and even loss. This lesson causes us to re-examine our view of suffering and discipline. Joseph' bizarre journey through the slave market and the dungeon finally led to a second in command position in that great Egyptian culture. The faith of Daniel's friends grew as they experienced God's deliverance in a furnace heated seven times hotter than it should have been. Daniel's faith grew as he was dropped into a den of lions, not a lion's den. Suffering is painful, but good can come from it. What trials are you experiencing right now? Do you need to change anything in how you face and reconcile yourself to where you are and where you want to be. Pray to be given the ability to see what God's plan is for you.

As we think about Christian suffering, we realize being a Christian isn't just sitting in a padded pew, listening and enjoying good singing, preaching, and church dinners in an air-conditioned building. Christian suffering takes you around the bend. You will find there no bed of roses. The glitter of Christian worship on television quickly fades. Are you a Christian and suffering? Do you have your own "thorn in the flesh?" Let the words of Daniel Sidney Warner, a holiness reformer who faced many heartaches in this life, encourage you in the midst of your suffering:

Who Will Suffer with the Savior?

Who will suffer with the Savior,
Take the little that remains
Of the cup of tribulation
Jesus drank in dying pains?

> Lord, we fellowship Thy passion,
> Gladly suffer shame and loss;
> With Thy blessing pain is pleasure,
> We will glory in Thy cross.

Who will offer soul and body
On the altar of our God?
Leaving self and worldly mammon,
Take the path that Jesus trod?

O for consecrated service

'Mid the din of Babel strife!
Who will dare the truth to herald
At the peril of this life?

Soon the conflict will be over,
Crowns await the firm and pure;
Forward, then, we work and suffer,
Faithful to the end endure.

-Warner, Daniel Sidney and Ludolph Schroeder.
WORSHIP THE LORD: HYMNAL OF THE CHURCH
OF GOD, Warner Press, 691.

Prayer

Lord, are we truly willing to suffer with you? Are we truly consecrated to your service? Are we committed and dedicated? We read and learn about so many giants of the faith. They trusted you. Do we have the same experience as they? Who will suffer with the Savior? Help us to find this pleasure in pain and gladness to suffer shame and loss. Help us to glory in your cross. Amen.

Parting Thought
"It's Not Always Easy"

It's not always easy to smile and be nice,
When we are called to sacrifice.
It's not always easy to put others first,
Especially when tired and feeling our worst.
It's not always easy to do the Father's will,

It wasn't easy to climb Calvary's hill.
But we as His children, should learn to obey,
Not seeking our own but seeking His way.
It's not always easy to fight the good fight,
But it is always good and it is always right!

Vocabulary:

Goad: Stick, stimulus, prod, something that urges.

For further study on this unit ...

Preaching from Hebrews can help any preacher prepare practical sermons from the epistle to the Hebrews.

It contains:

-

A concise commentary on Hebrews.

-

A survey of how great preachers have applied the wisdom of Hebrews.

-

A collection of sermons on special occasions, based on Hebrews.

PREACHING FROM HEBREWS
by James Earl Massey

ISBN 9781593176648 $24.99
S&H $5.00

Great Pastor Appreciation Month Gift!

14 S. Queen Street • Mt. Sterling, KY 40353
1-800-765-2464 • rpublisher@aol.com
www.reformationpublishers.com

NOVEMBER 6, 2016 · WEEK 10

EVERYTHING IS BRAND NEW

Lesson: Revelation 21:1-8

Key Verse - Revelation 21:4

And God shall wipe away all tears from their eyes; and there shall be no more death, neither sorrow, nor crying, neither shall there be any more pain: for the former things are passed away.

Introduction and Background

As we begin our study, it may be helpful to know who the author of the Book of Revelation is. Theoretically, the author is Jesus, the recorder for the book tells us in verse number one:

1 The Revelation of Jesus Christ, which God gave unto him, to shew unto his servants things which must shortly come to pass; and he sent and signified it by his angel unto his servant John:
2 Who bare record of the word of God, and of the testimony of Jesus Christ, and of all things that he saw *(Revelation 1:1-2 – KJV)*

John is the recorder of the Revelation of Jesus Christ. This is the Apostle John, the brother of James, the sons of Zebedee (**ZEBB** uh dee), a Galilean fisherman, and his wife Salome (suh **LOW** mee). The Gospel of John, along with three other books of the New Testament, 1st, 2nd and 3rd John all come from the mind and heart of this beloved apostle. The setting is the tiny island of Patmos, where John has been exiled by Domitian, the ruling emperor of the Roman Empire. It is the 66th book of the Bible, which is the last book. Similar to portions of Ezekiel and Daniel, the book is filled with symbolism, poetry, and prophetic events, specifically about the end time. It is believed that John had been exiled to this tiny island, a barren, rocky place covering less than 14 square miles of area, to silence him. This took place during Domitian's 15-year reign, placing John there as punishment for conducting forbidden evangelistic work in the city of Ephesus.

The book of Revelation was written in a type of literature known as apocalyptic. That word does not mean a "world-wide catastrophe" as the news and movie crowd of our day make it out to be. This style of writing was often used during times of national danger and it was a veiled way of covering the meaning of the writing from the foreign powers and authorities that were oppressing the nation at the time. It could be readily understood by those of the Hebrew nation but was totally obscure and meaningless to those outside the house of Israel. This book reveals the hidden workings and plans of the Lord God Almighty in the midst of the church's trials and tribulations. It has been a book of hope and encouragement to the saints across nearly two thousand years, showing readers that evil will not triumph. There is a day of reckoning and evil and its author will be cast into the Lake of Fire *(Revelation 19:20; 20:10, 14-15).*

In our study for this month, hopefully these four lessons will increase our knowledge of and appreciation for this rich book. In the final chapters of the book, John is given a vision of the wedding of Christ and His bride, the church.

It's All New
Revelation 21:1-2

1 And I saw a new heaven and a new earth: for the first heaven and the first earth were passed away; and there was no more sea.
2 And I John saw the holy city, new Jerusalem, coming down from God out of heaven, prepared as a bride adorned for her husband. *KJV*

John begins this chapter with the vision of a new heaven and a new earth which parallels the prophecy of Isaiah 65:17-18. Some think this will be a restored and wholly cleansed version of God's creation, or, it will be an unused, fresh heaven and earth that replaces the one that was marred by sin and its effect. I believe it will be a completely new model. Let me give you this thought. Our great God reveals Himself to be a creating God. The Bible tells us that God spoke all that there is into being and with the creation of man on the sixth day He pronounced it all very good. Then on the seventh day He rested. Now, here comes the question, *"Did God, who is a creating God, cease to create any longer?"* In my mind I don't think so! I think He has kept right on creating after His rest. How many new creations has He made in the last 2000 years? When this world with its attendant planets, stars and solar systems pass away with a great noise and melt with a fervent heat and all that has been of this world dissolves away,

> 2 Peter 3:10-13
>
> But the day of the Lord will come as a thief in the night; in the which the heavens shall pass away with a great noise, and the elements shall melt with fervent heat, the earth also and the works that are therein shall be burned up.
>
> 11 Seeing then that all these things shall be dissolved, what manner of persons ought ye to be in all holy conversation and godliness,
> 12 Looking for and hasting unto the coming of the day of God, wherein the heavens being on fire shall be dissolved, and the elements shall melt with fervent heat?
> 13 Nevertheless we, according to his promise, look for new heavens and a new earth, wherein dwelleth righteousness.

could it be that the bride of Christ, the church now complete with all the saints of all time, then settles down with her eternal Bridegroom, Jesus Christ, on one of those new creations? Well, the final answer will have to wait until we get there, won't it? Then John tells us of a new "holy city" — a New Jerusalem — coming down from God Himself.

Jerusalem has been at the center of the Jewish religion since the time of King David. It has also held special significance for the Christian faith as well. Historically, it has been marred by division, fighting, death, and chaos. It is going to pass away with all the rest of this world and its trappings as stated in 2 Peter 3. In this vision John sees a New Jerusalem — presented as a bride — a virgin, untouched, untainted, pure, and presentable by the Father to His Son, Jesus Christ. God doesn't fix or make over the old Jerusalem! He presents a new Holy City. Who is that New Jerusalem? Who is this beautiful, untouched, pure, virgin bride?

The Scripture identifies her for all those who have eyes to see and ears to hear. Look at verses 9 and 10:

9 And there came unto me one of the seven angels which had the seven vials full of the seven last plagues, and talked with me, saying, Come hither, I will shew thee the bride, the Lamb's wife.
10 And he carried me away in the spirit to a great and high mountain, and shewed me that great city, the

holy Jerusalem, descending out of heaven from God,

These verses make it clear. Who is the Lamb? Jesus Christ! Who is the Lamb's wife? The church of God. The church is the New Jerusalem!

Our God Dwells
Revelation 21:3-5

3   And I heard a great voice out of heaven saying, Behold, the tabernacle of God is with men, and he will dwell with them, and they shall be his people, and God himself shall be with them, and be their God.
4   And God shall wipe away all tears from their eyes; and there shall be no more death, neither sorrow, nor crying, neither shall there be any more pain: for the former things are passed away.
5   And he that sat upon the throne said, Behold, I make all things new. And he said unto me, Write: for these words are true and faithful. *KJV*

Now that a new, holy, and perfect heaven and earth, and a New Jerusalem have been created, God is free to live among His people in that new heaven and new earth! When God "tabernacled" with the people in the wilderness *(Exodus 25:8)*, God's glory was always present. The pillar of fire hovered over the tabernacle by night and the pillar of cloud declared His presence through the day. When the cloud or the fire moved, the people packed and moved with the pillar of God's presence. This foreshadows the time coming in the new heaven and the new earth when God once again will live with His people. What a glorious concept!

All Done
Revelation 21:6-8

6 And he said unto me, It is done. I am Alpha and Omega, the beginning and the end. I will give unto him that is athirst of the fountain of the water of life freely.
7 He that overcometh shall inherit all things; and I will be his God, and he shall be my son.
8 But the fearful, and unbelieving, and the abominable, and murderers, and whoremongers, and sorcerers, and idolaters, and all liars, shall have their part in the lake which burneth with fire and brimstone: which is the second death. *KJV*

The One seated on the throne Revelation 21:5 now says,

> "It is DONE. I am Alpha and Omega, the beginning and the end. I will give unto him that is athirst of the fountain of the water of life freely"

This does not happen just by the natural flow of things. This happens and comes about only by the work of salvation wrought in this dark world by the coming of our eternal High Priest and Savior. The water spoken of springs from the well of salvation through the Alpha and the Omega who is the Son of God in human flesh comes where we are to save where we are from what we were! Salvation, peace, joy are just a few of the rewards of this great salvation.

On the other side of the coin are the curses levied against those whose practice and efforts run to evil. They will not be invited to take part in the new heaven and the new earth. Instead they will be separated from the saints and consign into the Lake of Fire *(v. 8)*. Speaking of this separation in another place *(Revelation 20:10 -14)*, John says twice that the ungodly will be "**cast**" into the Lake of Fire. The Greek word for "**cast**" is the word (bal'-lo) and the connotation is that of being hurled into that horrible pit. The picture of a baseball pitcher comes readily to mind, they are called hurlers. The lost will be physically hurled, thrown forcibly into that hellish maw. Look at the listing of those which will be thrown there, those whom the dregs of sin have sifted from that pool.

Conclusion

What a day it will be when we come to the place God has prepared for us. When He is fully present with us, we will no longer have to worry about those things that trouble us now. John's vision helps us to have a clearer picture. We believe that the promises of Revelation "are true and faithful" *(v. 5)* This chapter of Scripture looks forward to a time when the final victory has been fought; the Lamb of God is indeed victorious. Satan is forever vanquished along with his followers where they can never wage war on the saints again. And the most beautiful picture of all is God with His people. The Scripture has foretold of that day, but now it is a reality, it is here. In order to arrive there, where every believer is free to worship God without any hindrance, we must stay faithful to Christ here.

What a Day That Will Be

There is coming a day when no heartaches shall come,
No more clouds in the sky, no more tears to dim the eye;
All is peace forevermore on that happy golden shore—
What a day, glorious day, that will be.

What a day that will be when my Jesus I shall see,
And I look upon His face—the One who save me by His grace;
When He takes me by the hand, and leads me through the Promised Land,

What a day, glorious day, that will be.

There'll be no sorrow there, no more burdens to bear,
No more sickness, no pain, no more parting over there;
And forever I will be with the One who died for me—
What a day, glorious day, that will be.

Hill, Jim. WORSHIP THE LORD: HYMNAL OF THE CHURCH OF GOD, Warner Press, 243.

Prayer

What a day that will be! Thank you for the hope given to us. "We have a hope, brighter than the perfect day, God has given us His Spirit, and we want the world to hear it." We are grateful that salvation makes us a member of the church of God. We are in awe of the vision of John at our destination. Is that why John prayed, "Even so, come, Lord Jesus"? Amen.

Parting Thought

It is important to begin right,
but it is imperative to end well!

Vocabulary:

Apocalyptic, hurlers, dregs, and others the class may want to define.

NOVEMBER 13, 2016 · WEEK 11

I SEE A NEW JERUSALEM

Bible Passage: Revelation 21:9-14, 22–27

Key Verse - Revelation 21:22-23
And I saw no temple therein: for the Lord God Almighty and the Lamb are the temple of it. And the city had no need of the sun, neither of the moon, to shine in it: for the glory of God did lighten it, and the Lamb is the light thereof.

Introduction and Background

Last week John showed us the new heaven and the new earth coming down from God out of heaven. This reality will be free from all of the trouble, hurt, and pain of the former world which has disappeared with a great noise and dissolved away. Not even death will survive when the saints of God stand in the presence of the One Who will dwell with them forever. On the other hand, there will be judgment of those who have chosen to live contrary to the holiness desired and required of us by our God. These folks will experience another death, much different and more painful than the first death, because this one will separate them for all eternity from the presence of God and His people. This is called the second death *(Revelation 21:8)*. Cities of the ancient world were established with three primary concerns: access to water, access to trade routes, and defend ability. Regarding the last one, cities were usually built on high ground. Combined with the added height of a city's walls, this gave a strong tactical advantage to the defender of the city. Attackers had to advance uphill, making them easier targets for the archers to shoot arrows and hurl stone from atop of the ramparts.

A strong wall and gate system not only permitted an able defense, but deterred many would be attackers from even considering an attempt to conquer a city. Walls could be massive. Such was the case with Nebuchadnezzar's city of Babylon with walls 300 feet high and 80 feet thick at the base. All this helps us understand why John's vision reveals the new Jerusalem to be a city with tremendous walls and gates. John uses superlative terminology to describe the city. Using words describing ultimates (**streets of pure gold** – *Revelation 21:18*) and perfection (**cube shaped** – *Revelation 21:16*) are superlatives of imagery and speak to us of hyperbole (high **PERB** ah lee). These are not literal descriptions, they are symbolic imagery of spiritual things.

The language of the Revelation *(apocalypse)* is symbolic and not literal the way many people try to understand it in a literal sense. This is one of the reasons for some of the bizarre interpretations placed upon it. This veiled way of communicating through signs and symbols was used when the nation was in a precarious state or situation. During the Babylonian captivity Daniel used this kind of literature to communicate the message God gave him to his fellow countrymen. Ezekiel used it as well during his years of captivity in the visions he received and shared with others. That God wanted the message of the "**apocalypse**" preserved so as to not get lost at the fiat of some carnal passing power he couched it in a symbolic record. The book of Revelation is not meant to be understood literally. God gives you a key to its interpretation in Revelation chapter one in verse one. That is right out there isn't it? Let's look at it:

Revelation 1:1

> The Revelation of Jesus Christ, which God gave unto him, to shew unto his servants things which must shortly come to pass; and he sent and **signified** it by his angel unto his servant John: KJV

The word *signify* or *signified* means — To convey or express a meaning. Make known with a word or signal/sign. The word *symbol* means — an arbitrary sign (**written or printed**) that has acquired a conventional significance. Right there in verse number one of chapter number one God says that the Book of Revelation is a book of signs and symbols. That means that it is to be understood in the light of what the signs and or symbols represent and not in a natural literal fulfilment. So our search is to find the symbolic keys in the Scriptures and what they represent in the Scriptures.

To verify that this is sound instruction let Jesus demonstrate. John tells us of One who walked in the midst of the candlesticks who held seven stars in His right hand and wore the clothing of the High Priest *(Revelation 1:12 - 16)*. This is the resurrected, glorified Lord Jesus Christ. We know that literally He was not holding seven literal stars in His right hand nor is he standing on a seven branched golden candelabra. What do the stars and the candlesticks represent? Let Jesus speak:

Revelation 1:18-20

> 18 I am he that liveth, and was dead; and, behold, I am alive for evermore, Amen; and have the keys of hell and of death.
> 19 Write the things which thou hast seen, and the things which are, and the things which shall be hereafter;
> 20 The mystery of the seven stars which thou sawest in my right hand, and the seven golden candlesticks. The seven stars are the angels of the seven churches: and the seven candlesticks which thou sawest are the seven churches. *KJV*

Here we find that the stars are the angels or pastors of the churches and the candlesticks are the churches — a perfect example of signification from the lips of the

Master. Today's lesson sets about John describing this new heavenly city.

The Right Foundation
Revelation 21:9-14

9 And there came unto me one of the seven angels which had the seven vials full of the seven last plagues, and talked with me, saying, Come hither, I will shew thee the bride, the Lamb's wife.

10 And he carried me away in the spirit to a great and high mountain, and shewed me that great city, the holy Jerusalem, descending out of heaven from God,

11 Having the glory of God: and her light was like unto a stone most precious, even like a jasper stone, clear as crystal;

12 And had a wall great and high, and had twelve gates, and at the gates twelve angels, and names written thereon, which are the names of the twelve tribes of the children of Israel:

13 On the east three gates; on the north three gates; on the south three gates; and on the west three gates.

14 And the wall of the city had twelve foundations, and in them the names of the twelve apostles of the Lamb. *KJV*

John's vision complete – one of the seven angels which had the seven vials full of the seven last plagues, came to John and said; "Come hither, I will shew the bride, the Lamb's wife" (v.9). Let's deal with what is right up front. Notice the Lamb is written with a capital "L", that indicates that this is a messianic allusion. It is referring to the Messiah! Who is the Lamb? It is Jesus, the only begotten of the Father. Now, who is the bride of the Lamb? That can be none other than the church of God, the bride of Christ. So we see at the very outset that John is not talking about a "literal" physical city of building blocks and lumber and glass — he is talking about the "CHURCH" the bride of Christ! He goes on to describe her.

Verse ten states John was caught up in the spirit to a great and high mountain and God showed him that great city, the holy Jerusalem. If he was caught up in the spirit, then he saw a spiritual city. To see God's church, you have to be borne by the Spirit to a high place because God's church only lives in high places. The floods came in Noah's day, but Noah and his family were borne above the flood because they were on board the ark, which was a type of the church. It was designed and built according to God's divine plan. There was only one door in the side, one window in the top, it was pitched with pitch on the outside and on the inside, and it had no rudder or steering wheel.

So God's church is built according to God's plan, the door opened by the Roman spear in Jesus' side is our port of entry into God's church, she is saved by the blood, and sealed in sanctification by the blood or pitched by the blood outside and inside. She gets her orders from headquarters hence the window in the top for orders come down from heaven because that is where the Head of the church resides. When the waters receded from off the land, where did the ark come to rest? The ark landed on top of the mountains of Ararat. The Holy Spirit was her compass and Jesus Christ is her Captain and just as the ark was guided by God to the top of the mountain, so God's church is guided by the Holy Spirit high up on top of Mount Zion:

Hebrews 12:22-24

22 But ye are come unto mount Sion, and unto the city of the living God, the heavenly Jerusalem, and to an innumerable company of angels,
23 To the general assembly and church of the firstborn, which are written in heaven, and to God the Judge of all, and to the spirits of just men made perfect,
24 And to Jesus the mediator of the new covenant, KJV

Her walls are great and high, for they are walls of salvation, you cannot get around them, you cannot get over them, you cannot get under them, you have to come in at the door and Christ is the only door.

Living in God's Light
Revelation 21:21-27

21 And the twelve gates were twelve pearls; every

several gate was of one pearl: and the street of the city was pure gold, as it were transparent glass.

22 And I saw no temple therein: for the Lord God Almighty and the Lamb are the temple of it.

23 And the city had no need of the sun, neither of the moon, to shine in it: for the glory of God did lighten it, and the Lamb is the light thereof.

24 And the nations of them which are saved shall walk in the light of it: and the kings of the earth do bring their glory and honour into it.

25 And the gates of it shall not be shut at all by day: for there shall be no night there.

26 And they shall bring the glory and honour of the nations into it.

27 And there shall in no wise enter into it any thing that defileth, neither whatsoever worketh abomination, or maketh a lie: but they which are written in the Lamb's book of life. *KJV*

No sun or moon! In the church here we have the SUNlight *(Malachi 4:2)* of the New Testament which Jesus brought at His first coming. The moonlight was the Old Testament Scriptures that spoke of the Day of the Lord and the coming of Messiah. Dr. Lillie S. McCutcheon preached the Woman bright as the sun (the greater light, the New Testament) in Rev. 12 stands upon the moon (the lesser light, the Old Testament). The Old Testament is the New Testament concealed while the New Testament is the Old Testament revealed preached Dr. Boyce W.

Blackwelder. But when Jesus comes again, we will no longer need the Old Testament or a New Testament for God and His Son will be all the light we will ever need, timeless, with perfect knowledge and insight will be ours.

Twelve gates each of pearl. Man's number is six '6', but when the two witnesses '2', when the Word and the Spirit start working inside a man's heart it will turn that man into a 12 (6 X 2 = 12). If you take 12 X 12 you have the squared number of 144 and if you add the perfect number 1000 to that 144 you have 144,000 which is the symbolic number of all God's people through the ages (See Rev. 14:1). Back to the gates of pearl, the pearl is made when a grain of sand gets inside the shell of an oyster. It's jagged edges irritate and hurt the oyster so he secretes a substance that builds a shield around that grain of sand. It takes a long time and indescribable pain to make that pearl which is never touched by human hands but comes into being out of great pain and agony. So Jesus came to earth by virgin birth, never touched by human origin. He lived, taught, preached and went through great suffering to purchase a pearl of great price, the plan of salvation. It is through that plan of salvation that you enter into God's glorious church, the body of Christ. That pearl gate is the New Birth and any and all can and must come into the family of God by the New Birth.

She, God's church, is to look upon like a jasper stone. The jasper stone is a stone of light, a stone of fire (a diamond). God is the Light and He is a consuming fire in

His church. Jesus said, "I am the Light of the world." God's church is light like a city set high on a hill or a candle stick held high in a window. The foundation is built upon the prophets and the apostles and Jesus Christ is the Chief Cornerstone. The stones in the walls of salvation are those lively stones or saved individuals that are placed in the walls of salvation by the Holy Ghost. Truth is what holds them all in place. The streets are of pure gold. You only get gold by burning it in the furnace so that all that is not gold is burned away, that is sanctification. So gold is a symbol of purity and holiness and God's saints walk in holiness before the Lord. There are three gates to the North, three gates to the South, three gates to the West, and three gates to the East. "Whosoever will" can readily enter into God's church through the Father, the Son, and the Holy Ghost. John was seeing God's church. Have you ever seen God's church or are you looking for cinder blocks and cedar beams and Kentucky flagstone?

Conclusion

Christians can count on having their names written in the Lamb's book of Life. It may not be written on the foundation stones of the church of God but it can and will be written into the Lamb's book when you yield your life to the Lord of the church. As we consider John's words in our lesson today, we can celebrate the place we look forward to going to. But the good news is that we can experience the New Jerusalem right here through the bride of Christ, the New Jerusalem. Literal Israel had a capitol city, Jerusalem. This Israel is: "Behold Israel after the flesh..." (1 Corinthians 10:18). There is another Israel, born at Calvary, the kingdom of God: "And as many as walk according to this rule, peace be on them, and mercy, and upon the **Israel of God**" *(Galatians 6:16)*. This spiritual Israel has a capitol city too, it is the New Jerusalem. The New Jerusalem is the capitol of the kingdom of God and as saints we are part of God's kingdom and citizens of God's capitol city, the New Jerusalem, through the birth of the Spirit. By providing us with a glimpse of what happens in the end to the church, and to God's enemies, and to all of God's children, we can be hopeful. The New Jerusalem, the prepared place, the praising place, the perfect place will be ours to enjoy fully. Thank God, however, all our eggs are not in one futuristic basket, we can rejoice, we can sing, we can live in victory here as part of the New Jerusalem and rest in the hope and knowledge that "We're moving on up!" when Jesus comes to gather His church and kingdom to ever be with Him.

Daniel Sidney Warner and Barney E. Warren with others traveled as part of the Flying Ministry days in the Church of God reformation movement. This allowed them time to compose and work on songs together. Here is a treasured old hymn of the church, *I Know My Name is There*:

My name is in the book of life,
O bless the name of Jesus!
I rise above all doubt and strife

And read y title clear.

    I know, I know my name is there;
    I know, I know my name is written there.
With sinners lost my name once stood
Upon a painful record;
But now it's canceled by the blood,
And written on His roll.

Yet inward trouble often cast
A shadow o'er my title;
But now with full salvation blest,
Praise God, it's ever clear!

While others climb thru worldly strife
To carve a name of honor,
High up in heaven's book of life,
My name is written there.

-Warner, Daniel S. and Barney E. Warren. WORSHIP THE LORD: HYMNAL OF THE CHURCH OF GOD, Warner Press, 435.

Prayer

    Lord, we are glad that we know our name is recorded in the Lamb's book of Life. We thank you that we see the church. We see beyond denominations, brick and mortar. We see all of the saved, the great family of God, the church of God! What a beautiful bride she is. Come and get her Lord when she is ready. Amen.

Parting Thought
Whoever does not have some foretaste of heaven' divine banquet here will never taste or partake of it there.

Vocabulary:
Fiat: Noun for decree, sanction, order.

NOVEMBER 20, 2016 · WEEK 12

LIVING WATERS

Bible Passage: Revelation 22:1-7

Key Verse - Revelation 22:1

And he shewed me a pure river of water of life, clear as crystal, proceeding out of the throne of God and of the Lamb.

Introduction and Background

Chapter 22 of Revelation is a message of divine invitation. The Spirit and the Bride say "Come." Everyone hearing and believing the message through God's written Word, and the pleading of Christ's church should be come to Christ and partake of the water of life freely. Here at the end of the book of Revelation is the new beginning where there are the new heavens and the new earth. As our study of Revelation 22 continues, the imagery of these opening verses takes us all the way back to the Creation as the story is told in the opening chapters of Genesis.

The beauty of God's Creation, its goodness and its perfection is mesmerizing just reading about it in Genesis 1 - 2. God made a Garden there that had everything that Adam would ever need. Adam wanted for nothing. Neither was there any occasion for hardship or suffering. It is a totally different story for those of us who live on this side of Genesis 3. Surrounded, as we are in this world, by sin and by unimaginable suffering and pain of every kind, we can see clearly what Adam had in the Garden, on the other side of Genesis 3 and what he lost — and what we lost — as the sons of Adam, in the impulsive decision of Adam and Eve. They threw it all away for a bite of the forbidden fruit.

Now, at the end of the way the Messiah has come. He has lived among us and taught, wrought miracles, been rejected and scorned by men and ultimately put to the cruelest death known to mankind of that day. But out of that tragedy of the crucifixion a new nation has been born and a new kingdom has been launched through His shed blood. True to the prophecy of Isaiah 2:2:

> "And it shall come to pass in the last days, that the mountain of the Lord's house shall be established in the top of the mountains, and shall be exalted above the hills; and all nations shall flow unto it" KJV.

The "mountain of the Lord's house" was to be established during the "last days". The Hebrew writer records in Hebrews 1:1 – 2 that: "God, who at sundry times and in divers manners spake in time past unto the fathers by the prophets, Hath in these *last days* spoken unto us by his Son, whom he hath appointed heir of all things, by whom also he made the worlds;" *KJV*.

Jesus was the fulfilment of that prophecy and true to Isaiah's words Jesus, the Messiah, came in "the last days" The last days started with His Advent. Jesus said in Matthew 5:17 that He came not to destroy the law, but to fulfil. When He died on the cross He cried, "It Is Finished!" *(John 19:30)*. What is finished? First, He spoke of the work His Father sent Him to do *(John 17:4)*, next to fulfil the law. With His resurrection on the third day, He brought to completion the fulfilment of the Law and the prophets. The "mountain of the Lord's house" had been established and "the New Jerusalem", the church – the bride of Christ, had been born through His shed blood. Hear the Hebrew writer as he speaks of the "mountain of the Lord's house" and of the bride at the top of the mountain:

Hebrews 12:22-23

But ye are come unto mount Sion, and unto the city of the living God, the heavenly Jerusalem, and to an innumerable company of angels, To the general assembly and church of the firstborn, *KJV*

With the death of the testator all of the stipulations of the testament (Will) kick in and precede any and all that was written before the testator's death *(Hebrews 9:16-17)*. This all took place at Calvary and on Resurrection Sunday! With the coming of the Holy Ghost on the

Day of Pentecost the "kingdom of God (mountain of the Lord's house)" was established above all the mountains (religions,religious systems of men) and the hills (denominations) of men. True to Jesus' words those standing there when He spoke them *(Mark 9:1)* saw the "kingdom of God" come with power and God began to add to the church such as should be saved *(Luke 16:16, Acts 2:38)*.

In today's lesson we have now come full circle. The reversal of the curse that God placed on the First Adam because of disobedience is about to be lifted by the obedience of the Last Adam, Jesus Christ. The hard labor that is required of man in this life is about to pass away, as will the curse upon the ground *(Genesis 3:17- 19)*. He is about to gather His New Jerusalem, His bride to His Father's house. A great celebration is at hand.

Perpetual Renewal
Revelation 22:1-2

1. And he shewed me a pure river of water of life, clear as crystal, proceeding out of the throne of God and of the Lamb.
2. In the midst of the street of it, and on either side of the river, was there the tree of life, which bare twelve manner of fruits, and yielded her fruit every month: and the leaves of the tree were for the healing of the nations. *KJV*

John's angel guide directs John's attention to the river

of life. This crystal clear river flowed from under the throne of God and the Lamb down the middle of the street. This means that John's final discovery is that of the redemption that flows from the throne of God. The last sign is the sign of hope. Jesus Christ is able to forgive and heal; the One who heals is the One who also reigns and therefore, the healing of this Lamb has authority. It lasts. Jesus Christ, the Lamb/Shepherd, is able to keep His sheep here and hereafter, to sustain them for all time. Where did John draw such imagery? Read Ezekiel's vision in Ezekiel 47. There Ezekiel sees a river of life-giving water that flowed from the restored temple southward into the Dead Sea, which became fresh and swarmed with fish; and along its banks grew trees bearing a new crop for each month of the year and the leaves had curative properties. The parallels are obvious with Revelation 11:1-2. Here the water flows from the throne and not the temple. The metaphor is the same though — the water of life flows from the presence of God. This water is symbolic of salvation, eternal life. We possess eternal life here and we live and move and have our being in God and among His children, the body and bride of Christ. We don't have to wait until we get to that heavenly clime to enjoy eternal life, we have it as a present reality if we have conducted business with our High Priest.

The woman at the well of Sychar found this living water. Jesus told her in John 4:13-14, "...Whosoever drinketh of this water shall thirst again. But whosoever drinketh of the water that I shall give him shall never thirst; but the water that I shall give him shall be in him a well of water springing up into everlasting life." Daniel Sidney Warner wrote of this living water in song:

River of Peace

I'll sing of a river divine,
Its waters from trouble release;
More precious than "honey and wine,"
That river, sweet river is peace.

'Tis flowing from heaven to earth,
It issues from under the throne;
Great peace! O thy infinite worth!
Sweet peace in my Jesus alone.

O wonderful life-giving flood,
Thy waters so crystal and pure
Make glad all the "City of God";
Forever thy blessings endure.

O Jesus! the tempest of sin
Is hushed into heavenly rest
Since tasting the pure living stream
That flows from Thy crucified breast.

My moments, as angels appear,
All gliding so gently along,
Each dropping a blessing so rare,
Enraptures my soul with a song.

O this river of peace
Makes me perfect and whole;
And its blessings increase,
Flowing deep in my soul.

-Warner, Daniel Sidney and Barney W. Warren. WORSHIP THE LORD: HYMNAL OF THE CHURCH OF GOD, Warner Press, 485.

Only God would have this kind of patience, waiting thousands of years to put into action His eternal plan to send His Son to die on our behalf. When the time was right *(Galatians 4:4),* Jesus was born of a woman to redeem those that were under the law. In like manner when the time is right Jesus will return to take His New Jerusalem, His bride to meet the Father and to the *"marriage supper of the Lamb."*

Ponder Points

What are some ways that you can be a vessel through which the *"water of life"* can flow through you that others may get a taste of it? Have you encountered people who are thirsty for something more than what they have? Do you make serving Jesus attractive to them?

Permanent Access
Revelation 22:3-5

3   And there shall be no more curse: but the throne of God and of the Lamb shall be in it; and his servants shall serve him:

4 And they shall see his face; and his name shall be in their foreheads.

5 An there shall be no night there; and they need no candle, neither light of the sun; for the Lord God giveth them light: and they shall reign for ever and ever. *KJV*

This passage starts "no more curse." When we get to the eternal world, the curse will be lifted. The saints will have the seal of the Father's name upon their heads and God and His Son will be the light causing darkness to be banished forever. That will be the conditions of our status in eternity. Without question it is going to be a glorious blessing and adventure to see our heavenly Father and our blessed Redeemer and have access to the river of life when that time arrives. But, we still have to live in the now until that time does arrive when the Bridegroom comes for His bride.

The knowledge that Jesus, our eternal Redeemer, is able to deliver His sheep and to keep His sheep eternally is our real authority in the world. Just as the authority of a professor in a class meeting is not established by his academic title but by the truth of his lecture, so, in the same way, the authority of the church depends upon the authority and truth of the Gospel we preach about Jesus Christ and His promises. John is closing this final passage with his vision of that ultimate authority.

This has very practical application and implications:

the reason a child of God does not despair in the midst of the sinfulness and confusion of the world in which they live is because of the tree of (the vine -- John 15:5) life and the water *(John 4:14; John 6:35)* that heals. Because of that living hope, there is no person or situation that is hopeless. Drug addiction, racial hatreds, gross immorality and self- indulgence, and all other sins of every shade and hue can be healed by the Redeemer Jesus Christ. Equally important is the fact that Christ can begin here and now and it can last for all time until time gives way to eternity. The only sin that cannot be healed is the sin of unbelief that refuses the convicting work of the Holy Spirit that does not want the forgiveness of the Lamb. However, if we repent and open the door of our heart, the Lamb will come in and sup with us and we with Him. Now in the vision of that eternal gathering into God's dining room for the Marriage Supper of the Lamb, we have discovered what a party awaits all of the saints of all of the ages. The journey of the Bible is a journey from the Word of God to the Word of God...a journey from the Garden of Eden to the eternal city and garden of God.

Conclusion

The human race must continue to live in this imperfect world of injustice, oppression, pain, sickness and misery. God provides opportunity to right wrongs and reverse injustice through legal, political, and social means. However, we must avoid the pitfall of seeing social and political reform as our catch all cure and become an idol, causing bitterness and disenchantment when cruelty and oppression continue. The cure for this world's plight and man's dilemma is not political, nor social, it is spiritual. The hearts of men and women must be changed to change the world. To hope for an earthly paradise is a pipe dream for it will never happen. The Christian's hope is upon a higher plain. John has placed it before us. In the new heavens and new earth, God's bride, the church, stands radiantly atop Mount Zion and the New Jerusalem where-in lies true and eternal healing for any and all. The Holy Spirit reminds us, through John's vision, that even as we seek to see the Gospel transform our society in the here and now, follow the admonition of the apostle Paul to the Colossians and to us:

Colossians 3:1

> If ye then be risen with Christ, seek those things which are above, where Christ sitteth on the right hand of God.

When We All Get to Heaven

Sing the wondrous love of Jesus,
Sing His mercy and His grace;
In the mansions bright and blessed
He'll prepare for us a place.

> *When we all get to heaven,*
> *What a day of rejoicing that will be!*
> *When we all see Jesus,*
> *We'll sing and shout the victory!*

While we walk the pilgrim pathway
Clouds will overspread the sky;
But when traveling days are over
Not a shadow, not a sigh.

Let us then be true and faithful,
Trusting, serving every day;
Just one glimpse of Him in glory
Will the toils of life repay.

Onward to the prize before us!
Soon His beauty we'll behold;
Soon the pearly gates will open—
We shall tread the streets of gold.

Hewitt, Eliza E. and Emily D. Wilson. WORSHIP THE LORD: HYMNAL OF THE CHURCH OF GOD, Warner Press, 729.

Prayer

Lord, we anticipate all that you have prepared for us. When the disciples were troubled, You said, "Let not your hearts be troubled." Help us to remember those words today. We face many troubles here. Some refugees have left war at home. Some grandparents are raising grandchildren due to drugs. Some are going for cancer treatments. Some are in prison. All of this is temporary. Help us to remember that this body goes back to the dust from whence it came and the spirit, the soul return to You. Amen.

Parting Thought

Old Brother George had a long, hard illness. On his last day alive, someone came to him and said, *"How are you doing?"* He said, *"I'm almost well."*

NOVEMBER 27, 2016 · WEEK 13

ALPHA AND OMEGA

Bible Passage: Revelation 22:11- 21

Key Verse - Revelation 22:13
I am Alpha and Omega,
the beginning and the end,
the first and the last.

Introduction and Background

The book of Revelation is the last book of the New Testament and the sixty-sixth book of the Bible. It is the consummation of biblical prophecy disclosing the future of the Jewish nation, the Gentiles, and the church of God, the bride of Christ. This great prophetic unfolding deals mainly with the events preceding the second coming of Jesus, and final things that usher in the eternal state. The name of the book comes from the Greek *apokalypsis* meaning *"an unveiling"; "the removing of a veil."* So it goes without saying that this is a book written to be understood. The book is not correctly called the Revelation of the apostle John. It is precisely "the Revelation of Jesus Christ" *(Revelation 1:1)*. That is, it is an unveiling of His future plan for the earth and for His redeemed saints both for time and eternity. It is necessary to view the book as in no sense sealed *(Revelation 22:10)*. A distinct blessing is promised to the person that reads it and to those who hear the words of its prophecy *(Revelation 1:3)*. If you could not understand it how could you keep the things written therein and how could you be blessed by it? It is simply uninformed chatter to say that God does not intend this book to be understood or that the symbolism and figures of the prophecy are incomprehensible. The figures and symbols of the book, which furnish the basis of its interpretation, are found elsewhere in the other 65 books of the Bible and can only be understood in the light of coherent and connected comparative study of all other lines of prophecy and prophetic type and symbolism. "Search the scriptures; for in them ye think ye have eternal life: and they are they which testify of me" *(John 5:39 KJV)*.

Interpretation of the book demands a thorough acquaintance with all the other great prophecies that merge in this book, which is like a great spiritual Train Station where the trunk lines of all the trains of prophecy come in from all of the other Scriptures and are meshed together in a glorious tapestry of truth about God's plan, God's provision, God's people, God's High Priest (**Jesus Christ**) and the Paradise of God which is to come. John lived in a time when Rome was the dominant political power of the world of that day. He specifically names himself as the author of Revelation, and he writes with authority to the church as a whole, Jew and Gentile. From reading the Gospels we know he is one of the sons of Zebedee along with his brother James who were nicknamed by Jesus as the "**Sons of Thunder.**" John had a close relationship with Jesus, the Messiah. On at least three different occasions John, along with James, his brother, and Peter spent blocks of time alone with Jesus and apart from the other nine apostles *(Luke 8:51; Matthew 17:1; Mark 14:33)*.

Eschatology (**ES** kha taw low gee), drawn from the Greek word *eschatos* (**ES**'-khat-os – final things, time of the end), is the study of end time things and in particular death, judgment and the eternal realms of heaven and hell. Both Revelation in the New Testament and Daniel in the Old Testament are books that prophesy that the end is imminent. The return of Jesus is a central subject of this type of study and the book of Revelation is a case in point. In the last verses of Revelation, John assures his readers of the certainty of Christ's return. We have read the letters to the seven churches, the opening of the seven seals, the sounding of seven trumpets, the pouring out of seven bowls in judgment. As John writes, each time one of the seven angels holding the seven bowls has been John's spiritual guide.

Alpha and Omega
Revelation 22:12-13

12 And, behold, I come quickly; and my reward is with me, to give every man according as his work shall be.

13 I am Alpha and Omega, the beginning and the end, the first and the last. *KJV*

The "I AM" statements from the book of Exodus *(3:13-15)* come to mind when Jesus declares "I AM" Alpha and Omega!" God instructed Moses to tell the people of Israel that God sent him. Moses asked God for a specific name, and God's response is, "I AM THAT I AM," that is it, "I am everything and whatever is required at any given moment of time" Jesus employs the "I AM" statement as to the connection He has with God Who is ALL in ALL. When it speaks of "my reward is with me," the text literally reads one who brings *"wages"*. Yes, payday, is coming! In Jesus' hand is either punishment for those who rejected Him as Lord and Savior or reward for those who accept Him as the only means for salvation. Everyone must make the right decision and must prepare, since the certainty of the Lord's return is before us.

After announcing His return, Jesus again identifies Himself. He uses the first letter of the Greek alphabet, "Alpha" and the last letter of the Greek alphabet, "Omega", which is equivalent to saying "I am the 'A' and I am the 'Z', and I am everything in between!" Jesus uses the same form of identity four times throughout Revelation *(Revelation 1:8, 11; 21:6; 22:13)*.

City Gates
Revelation 22:14-15

14 Blessed are they that do his commandments, that they may have right to the tree of life, and may enter in through the gates into the city.

15 For without are dogs, and sorcerers, and whoremongers, and murderers, and idolaters, and whosoever loveth and maketh a lie. *KJV*

There is a certain entry point for those who receive the promises detailed in the book of Revelation. The blessings that are offered are gained when one does the commandments of God *(v. 14)*. The one who does these commandments has access to the New Jerusalem and a right to the tree of life and to drink of the water of life. They have access to the blessings God has for those who love Him. Jesus is the entry point, He is that "**pearly gate**" through which we must pass to enter into the city. Remember the story of the pearl made inside an oyster through great pain and agony. A stone never touched by human hands? Jesus is that "**pearl of great price**" born of a virgin, suffering and dying on a cruel cross to give us entrance through the "**New Birth**" into the household of God! Glory!

Outside the gates, however, are dogs. Recall the conversation between Jesus and the Canaanite (**CANE un ite**) woman whose daughter was sick (Matthew 15:21-28). Confronted by her, Jesus told her that it was not right to take the children's food and throw it to the dogs. To this the woman replied, "...Truth, Lord: yet the dogs eat of the crumbs which fall from their masters' table" *(Matthew 15:27 – KJV)*. The list continues with sorcerers and fornicators and murderers and idolaters, and everyone who loves and practices lying. Once the gate is closed, there is no more opportunity to come inside the city. When Jesus returns the gate will be officially closed!

The Invitation
Revelation 22:16-18

16 I Jesus have sent mine angel to testify unto you these things in the churches. I am the root and the offspring of David, and the bright and morning star.

17 And the Spirit and the bride say, Come. And let him that heareth say, Come. And let him that is athirst come. And whosoever will, let him take the water of life freely. *KJV*

Jesus is both the Source and the Root of David. Without Him, David would not have been! Recall the words of Isaiah 11 – " **a shoot shall come out from the stump of Jesse, and a Branch shall grow out of his roots.**" Next, Jesus says He is the Light in a world of darkness, He is the "**bright and morning star**" *(Revelation 22:16)*. He is the beginning of a bright new eternal day!

Next comes a clear invitation *(Revelation 22:17)*. Here is great encouragement to any who may read this book and who may now desire to meet the Lamb. The Holy Spirit is joined with "the bride", the church, in calling out the words of generous encouragement and invitation to all who are thirsty. The Isaiah prophecy comes to mind, "Ho, every one that thirsteth, come ye to the waters, and he that hath no money; come ye, buy, and eat; yea, come, buy wine and milk without money and without price" *(Isaiah 55:1– KJV).*

The Warning
Revelation 22:18-21

18 For I testify unto every man that heareth the words of the prophecy of this book, If any man shall add unto these things, God shall add unto him the plagues that are written in this book:

19 And if any man shall take away from the words of the book of this prophecy, God shall take away his part out of the book of life, and out of the holy city, and from the things which are written in this book.

20 He which testifieth these things saith, Surely I come quickly. Amen. Even so, come, Lord Jesus.

21 The grace of our Lord Jesus Christ be with you all. Amen. *KJV*

The book concludes with a warning like that of a wedding, "Those whom God has joined together let no man put asunder." The book's ending is a warning to the readers not to tamper with the record of the visions of Jesus given to John. We are to stand reverently before and beneath God's Word. We do not look over the Bible's shoulder to correct its theology; it is rather that the Bible corrects our theology! The book ends as it began — with the first love that comes from the Lord Jesus Christ. The book ends with the assurance of the faithfulness and steadfastness of that love. Amen! Here is the Rock upon which to build your life: the faithfulness of the love of Jesus Christ. It will endure forever!

Conclusion

Our quarter ends with this final lesson on the final chapter of the final book. The theme "**Alpha and Omega,**" supports the lessons from Isaiah and the letter to the Hebrews, which focused on the sovereignty of the Father and of the Son. Jesus clearly is Lord, and He IS the "**Alpha**" and the "**Omega**". He is returning to claim His own, and He will bring His reward with Him. He did not come today, but I look for Him tonight. If He allows me to see the light of another day, I will be looking for Him tomorrow. In the midst of heartache, and heartbreak, with the chaos, turmoil, terrorism, mayhem on our streets there is a part of me that longs for His coming, but for those of my loved ones who are lost, and the myriads who need Jesus as Savior, my heart pleads "**wait a little longer, please Jesus.**"

Be Ready When He Comes

Would you flee from sin and serve the Lord?
Be ready when He comes;

He will soon appear with His reward,
Be ready when He comes.

It is not His will that you be lost,
Be ready when He comes;
Would you save your soul at any cost?
Be ready when He comes.

Do you know the end of time is near?
Be ready when He comes;
Soon the Lord to judge us shall appear;
Be ready when He comes.

There is awful danger in delay,
Be ready when He comes;
Will you cast your only hope away?
Be ready when He comes.

Be ready, Be ready, Be ready when He comes;
Be ready, Be ready, Be ready when He comes.

-Teasley, D. Otis. WORSHIP THE LORD: HYMNAL OF THE CHURCH OF GOD, Warner Press, 384.

Prayer

Lord, John was ready for You to come. Help us to be ready for You to come. Help us get as many as we can ready for Your coming. Help our missionaries to win the nations to You. We need Your divine help to reach this generation. Amen.

Parting Thought

There is an inscription in the dome of our Capitol in Washington which few people know about. It says: *"One far-off divine event toward which the whole creation moves."* A visitor saw this inscription and asked the guide what it meant. He said, *"I think it refers to the Second Coming of Jesus Christ."* Our founding Fathers believed that God and Christ were integral to the successful development of the nation. They had the wisdom to place this inscription in the dome of our Capitol Building at its construction.

For further study ...

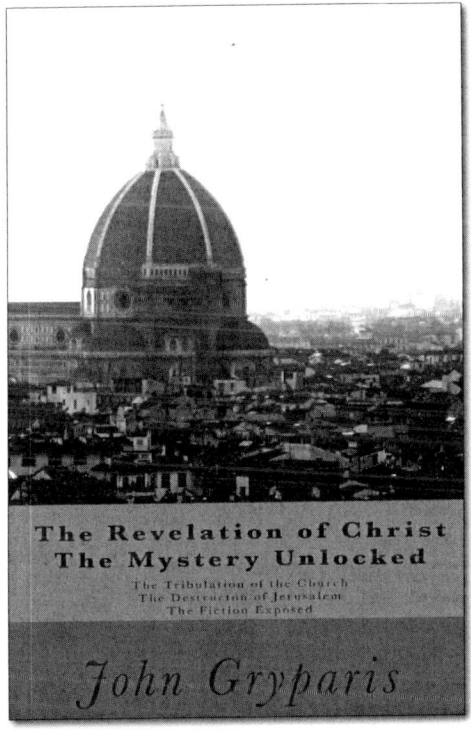

THE REVELATION OF CHRIST: THE MYSTERY UNLOCKED
by John Gryparis

ISBN 9781469918358 Softcover $15

S&H $5

REFORMATION PUBLISHERS

14 S. Queen Street • Mt. Sterling, KY 40353
1-800-765-2464 • rpublisher@aol.com
www.reformationpublishers.com

For further study ...

SCENES FROM THE THRONE
by Richard M. Bradley

ISBN 9781933304052 Softcover $20
ISBN 9781933304557 Hardcover $25
S&H $5

REFORMATION PUBLISHERS

14 S. Queen Street • Mt. Sterling, KY 40353
1-800-765-2464 • rpublisher@aol.com
www.reformationpublishers.com

For further study ...

TWO VIEWS OF THE MILLENNIUM
by Douglas J. Simpson and Wade T. Jernigan

ISBN 0892658746 Softcover $15
S&H $5

14 S. Queen Street • Mt. Sterling, KY 40353
1-800-765-2464 • rpublisher@aol.com
www.reformationpublishers.com

For further study ...

A CASE FOR AMILLENNIALISM
by Kim Riddlebarger

ISBN 9780801064357 Softcover $21.99
S&H $5

REFORMATION PUBLISHERS

14 S. Queen Street • Mt. Sterling, KY 40353
1-800-765-2464 • rpublisher@aol.com
www.reformationpublishers.com

For further study ...

THE SYMBOLS SPEAK
by Dr. Lillie S. McCutcheon

ISBN 1933304243 Softcover $15
ISBN 9781604163018 Hardcover $25
S&H $5

REFORMATION PUBLISHERS

14 S. Queen Street • Mt. Sterling, KY 40353
1-800-765-2464 • rpublisher@aol.com
www.reformationpublishers.com

For further study ...

THE FUTURE:
AN AMILLENNIAL PERSPECTIVE
by Cecil Sanders

ISBN 0892651407 Softcover $15

S&H $5

REFORMATION PUBLISHERS

14 S. Queen Street • Mt. Sterling, KY 40353
1-800-765-2464 • rpublisher@aol.com
www.reformationpublishers.com